The Farming Joke Book

A collection of agricultural jokes,
amusing stories and anecdotes

John Terry

Old Pond
PUBLISHING

By the same author
Pigs in the Playground
Calves in the Classroom
Ducks in Detention
Rabbits on Report
How to Become a First-Generation Farmer

The Farming Joke Book

A collection of agricultural jokes,
amusing stories and anecdotes

John Terry

*Hon. BA., Cert.Ed., C. Biol., M.R.S.B.,
M.C.I.Hort., F.R.Ag.S., F.R.S.A.*

First published 2015

Copyright © John Terry 2015

All rights reserved. No part of this publication may be reproduced,
stored in a retrieval system, or transmitted, in any form or by any means,
electronic, mechanical, photocopying, recording or otherwise, without
prior permission of the copyright holder.

Published by
5M Publishing Ltd,
Benchmark House,
8 Smithy Wood Drive,
Sheffield, S35 1QN, UK
Tel: +44 (0) 1234 81 81 80
www.5mpublishing.com

A catalogue record for this book is available from the British Library

ISBN 978-1-910456-11-8

Book layout by Servis Filmsetting Ltd, Stockport, Cheshire
Printed by Bell & Bain
Illustrations by Rory Walker

*For my lovely wife Sarah and our two wonderful children
Jonathan and Roseanna and not forgetting
my dear mother and father.*

Acknowledgements

My wife Sarah has been wonderful reading through the manuscript and taking on the enormous task of typing it up on the computer.

Contents

About the author

John Terry has always been interested in farming. He was brought up by his parents on a private housing estate in Nuneaton, Warwickshire. At weekends and during school holidays he stayed with his uncle and aunt on a 500 acre farm in Leicestershire. His uncle was a farm manager and both his uncle and aunt were real country people and taught John a great deal about farming and wildlife. Living at home with his parents John was lucky to be able to keep many pets including a dog of his own and he kept and showed rabbits, guinea pigs, bantams and cage birds. He has always had an excellent sense of humour and enjoys telling jokes (like his father did) and over the years has given over 500 amusing talks and after dinner speeches.

As he grew older he became a member of Nuneaton Young Farmer's Club and over the years became treasurer, chairman, club leader and president. After leaving school he worked full time on a farm for a year before completing a three year college course at Worcester College of Education (now the University of Worcester) to become a Rural Studies teacher. He became head of Rural Studies at Higham Lane School, Nuneaton (the school he attended as a boy) and developed a thriving school farm and gardens, keeping calves, sheep, goats, chickens, ducks, geese and two Jersey cows purchased as calves from HM the Queen. In fact, the highlight of his teaching career was a visit to the school by HM the Queen and the Duke of Edinburgh.

John taught for 25 years at the school and during this time wrote four amusing books about his life on the school farm. In 1989 he purchased a field that had not been farmed for a number of years with no electricity, no farm buildings and a very poor water supply. The field was soon cultivated, grassed and a poultry unit installed for free range laying hens. Over the years the poultry enterprise has increased to 5000 birds. In addition, both pedigree Kerry Hill and Derbyshire Gritstone sheep have been bred and shown, winning numerous championships including the Champion Flock of Kerry Hill sheep in Britain and the Champion of Champions award with a Derbyshire Gritstone ram. Kerry Hill sheep have been exported to Holland and Kerry Hill semen exported to the USA. John is also a top sheep judge, judging major shows in Britain plus shows in Ireland and Holland. He has written an excellent text book entitled *How to Become a First-Generation Farmer* which has proved popular with new farmers and established farmers. He was awarded Fellowship of the Royal Agricultural Society (F.R.Ag.S.) in 1993.

John's enthusiasm, determination, intelligence, humour and excellent communication skills have been apparent in all his endeavours as he has proven himself to be a good farmer, establishing a farm of which he can be proud. John is good at getting what he wants – he gained planning permission for a mobile home on his site which he lived in before he got planning permission for a permanent bungalow. Over the years the farmland has increased to 13.92 hectares (34.5 acres) and now includes a field to grow arable crops. He has always led an integrated life, formerly close to his parents and now close to his wife Sarah and their children Jonathan and Roseanna. His family are involved in everything he does.

Cattle

If you pampered your cow too much what would you expect to get?

Spoilt milk.

I witnessed one of my students pick up a calf's tail and immediately kiss the calf directly under the base of the tail.

I asked, "What are you doing that for?"

"I've got chapped lips," was his reply.

"Well, that won't cure them," I said, sternly.

"No, Sir, but it stops me licking them."

What do you call a bull that keeps dropping off to sleep?

A bulldozer.

When an American visitor from Texas visited my school and looked over the cattle shed door where we kept two Hereford calves he said to my students, "I see you keep Hereford cattle in England, too, do you?"

One of my twelve year old students, Paul, who was from a towny background, was very quick to give him the origin and history of the breed – needless to say I was very proud of him. However, the American was not to be outdone. He asked my students, "How many acres have you got on this little old spread?"

"Just one acre," said Joe, proudly.

The American scoffed and said, "Don't make me laugh son – one acre isn't a farm. Back in Texas my garden is eight acres and my swimming pool is nearly an acre and when I get in my car at sun up I keep driving and driving and at sundown I still ain't reached the end of my land."

Joe replied, "Yes sir, we had a car like that once!"

Why do some cows have bells around their necks?

Because their horns don't work.

After our son Jonathan was born I got in the lift at the hospital and pressed the button for the ground floor. I immediately recognised an ex-student in the lift, it was Simon.

"Hello sir, are you a new dad?" he asked.

"Yes," I replied "Our first child – a boy, Jonathan."

"How about you?" I enquired.

"Yes, our first child, a girl but it took ages and ages for her to be born. We had two midwives and a doctor but it still took hours and hours, I'm exhausted! I said to the team — what are you messing about at? If my old Rural Studies teacher was here, Mr Terry, he would have got some lubricant and some calving ropes and the job would have been done in about twenty minutes."

"You didn't really say that did you?" I asked.

"Yes," he replied, "but my wife didn't like me saying it!"

"Well, I wouldn't have said it in front of my wife," I replied.

Why is the cowman happy at work in the milking parlour?

Because it is a place of udder delight.

A lovely pedigree black Aberdeen Angus bull was standing still in the centre of the road. A man driving his new Jaguar at 90 miles an hour approached the bull from around a very sharp bend. This lunatic driver had no side lights on and no headlights and not even any fog lights. Luckily he braked just in time to miss the bull. How did he miss killing or injuring the bull or indeed injuring himself?

Answer: It was daylight.

How does a cow creep out of a field and hardly get noticed?

Answer: Right pasteurise.

"You would look silly riding the cow," I replied.

Cattle

Cattle are expensive to buy and my old farm boss, Mo, was short of money.

"John, I don't know if I should buy a bicycle or a new Friesian cow," he pondered.

"You would look silly riding the cow," I replied.

"I would look even sillier trying to milk the bicycle," was his witty reply.

Why has a milking stool only got three legs?

The cow has the udder!

When I taught Rural Studies in a secondary school I was lucky to purchase a Jersey heifer called Windsor Coronets Crystal 6th from HM the Queen (and another calf at a later date).

I visited the Royal farm for the first time with a group of students. We were shown the calf but I worried how much money she would cost because she was just perfect. I asked the farm manager how much money the calf would be.

"The Queen can't give you the calf but we thought eighty pounds would be a fair price."

Eighty pounds! I could have dropped. Small cross bred calves at our local market fetched more than eighty pounds. I did not dare haggle the price. It was fair. Before I visited the farm I had visions of myself and Her Majesty getting our heads together and haggling, bartering with my usual currency – a dozen new laid eggs. The farm manager Trevor did not want paying there and then – the invoice would be sent to us. We all thanked Trevor very much indeed.

"You can have her for eighty pounds as long as you promise one thing – when it is time to breed with her don't take her to the nearest bull down the road."

One of my students, Diane's brow furrowed. "But why can't Mr Terry take her to the nearest bull down the road?" she asked in all innocence.

"Look, let me explain," said Trevor patiently. "It's the equivalent of Mr Terry taking Princess Anne out for the night. It's just not done."

"Well! That's put me in my place hasn't it?" I remarked.

What is a bullock with no legs called?
Ground beef.
What is a bullock with no back legs called?
Lean beef.

Funny stories are part of the armoury of many salesmen and the true ones are often the funniest. I heard a corker from Tom Hendrick after he had left some free substitute calf milk and a thermometer with Mo, my old farm boss, whose unenlightened ways were something of a legend in the area. The thermometer was fixed to a flat rectangular piece of plastic with a small handle on top, the whole thing being about 15cm long and 5cm wide. A week later the rep called to see how Mo was getting on with the milk.

"The milk is very good," Mo said, "but I couldn't get on with that damn thermometer – it was really hurting the poor calves".

It transpired that Mo had not used the gadget for testing the milk. He had been taking the temperature of the calves with it and as you do not place a thermometer under a calf's tongue it was little wonder they were not very happy with the operation.

When we castrate our bull calves they are sure to weigh two stones lighter!

A farming couple I know very well built their new calf building far too close to the house which attracted flies into their house during the summer.

"I'm fed up with these flies in the house," she yelled. Her husband was swatting them in the kitchen.

"I've just killed five" he reported. He went on to say, "Three males and two females."

"How do you know what sex they were?" she asked.

"Three were on the beer and two were on the telephone," was his reply.

"Well you won't believe this but he wears a brown paper bag hat, a brown paper bag shirt, brown paper bag trousers and even brown paper bag boots."

If your cow kicks your bucket of milk over don't cry over spilled milk, turn the udder cheek and move on.

In Texas when cowboys ruled the range, the sheriff and the deputy sheriff worked well together in their office and jail house.

"I've at last arrested the notorious criminal Brown Paper Bag Pedro," announced the sheriff excitedly.

"Why is he called Brown Paper Bag Pedro?" enquired the deputy sheriff.

"Well you won't believe this but he wears a brown paper bag hat, a brown paper bag shirt, brown paper bag trousers and even brown paper bag boots."

"So what have you arrested him for?"

"Rustling," was the sheriff's reply.

Two cows talking in a field:

One cow says to the other,

"What are your views on this mad cow disease?"

The other one replies, "It's no use asking me I'm a duck!"

An old farmer was milking his lovely old Jersey cow called Bluebell and he noticed a large fly go straight into the cow's ear. The fly then appeared as if by magic in the milking bucket. "Well, I can't believe this," thought the old farmer. "I've never seen that before so did the fly go in one ear and out the udder?"

A towny lady asked the farmer, "Why is the grass in this field so short?"

"The cows are all lawn moo-ers," was his reply.

My old farm boss, Mo, kept Friesians and did not like Jerseys one little bit. One of his farming neighbours, Cyril Webster, kept Jerseys and the arguments that ensued between these two on the merits of Friesians versus Jerseys often threatened to get out of hand although, no matter how heated the arguments, they always remained the best of friends.

"Friesian milk is nothing but water," sneered Cyril.

"Rubbish! Friesian milk is quite normal – but that Jersey milk is too damn rich and creamy for my liking," retorted Mo up in arms.

"I'll tell you what – you could place a ten pence piece on top of Jersey milk and it would stay there. The milk is almost solid but try putting it on top of Friesian milk and it will sink straight to the bottom. Not only that, if you peered over the top of the glass you would see the ten pence piece lying at the bottom. In fact, the milk is so watery I bet you could even read the date on it," remarked Cyril.

A couple of months later, mid-January to be exact, these two characters were in the pub again.

"My muck spreader's broken down can I borrow yours?" asked Mo.

"'Course you can," replied Cyril.

"I'll fetch it in the morning then".

Mo arrived early and started looking for Cyril. Cyril was still milking the cows. Mo went into the cowshed – it was the old fashioned sort – the cows being tethered by chains. As soon as he entered the shed Mo spotted it – a black and white Friesian tied up at the end of the line. It was immediately obvious to Mo that Cyril could not make the Jerseys pay and so had bought a Friesian. Mo's moment had arrived and he was going to milk it for all it was worth.

"What's this then, Cyril? Have you seen sense at last? Are you going to admit that your Jerseys don't pay?"

Cyril, however, was ready with a witty come-back.

"Well, I've been getting trouble with the water pipes freezing so I bought a Friesian. I thought I could milk her first then if the water in the pipes does freeze up I can use her milk to wash the cows' teats with." A brilliant answer but in the end Cyril lost because two years later he had sold every Jersey and kept nothing but Friesians.

The Warwickshire farmers annual dinner and dance is a grand affair with a wonderful meal and an old fashioned dance band. It has run for years and traditionally various awards are given out including prizes for the best crop of wheat in the district, the best potatoes, best dairy herd and best flock of sheep as well as individual awards given to farmers. Our local AI (artificial insemination) man is a grand fellow and I am pleased to say at last year's dinner he was awarded the 'Long Service' award.

During his thank you speech he was asked what qualifications he had, his quick reply was "A long arm."

A sign found on a Herefordshire farm read, 'It won't cost you any money to cross my land but my bull might charge.'

I enjoyed keeping a Jersey cow at school; educationally it was good to have a large dairy animal as well as our goats. Many lessons could be taught involving the cow from maths to art, English to Geography. However, one time after school my students forgot to milk her. "You students are so forgetful," I said sternly. "Come on, get her milked now!"

"We will, Sir, but on the other hand what kind of milk comes from a forgetful cow?" asked Jeremy.

"I've got no idea," I replied.

"Milk of amnesia, Sir!" was his reply. The whole group of students groaned.

One of my examination questions was "Explain how milk gets from the cow to the doorstep."

Answer: "Milk is delivered to the doorstep by dairies such as the Co-op and Urinate."

Susie had an iron cow
She milked it with a spanner
The milk comes out in shilling tins
The little ones a tanner.

Note: This rhyme was around before the decimalisation of money. A shilling is 10 pence and a tanner is 5 pence.

I was honoured that the Queen and the Duke of Edinburgh were to visit the school to see our school farm and above all to see the second Jersey that I purchased from the Queen – Windsor Grand Good News.

Sarah, our head girl, arrived at my classroom door.

"Hello, Sarah," I said cheerfully.

"Hello, Sir. The headmaster says I'm to present the Queen with a posy of flowers when she arrives tomorrow morning."

"That is a great honour," I said.

"I know, Sir, but what do I say to her?"

"'Good morning, Your Majesty, welcome to our school'"

"Thank you Sir. By the way, what does ER stand for?" she asked.

"Elizabeth Regina," I said.

"Well, can't I just say 'ere y'are ER?"

"No you most certainly cannot," I said emphatically.

Dairy farmer talking:

"I could dance with the wife until the cows came home soon after we got married and now I could dance with my cows until she doesn't come home!"

My farm boss said on a very cold morning, "John, my hands are so cold I thought I was milking Daisy but actually I was shaking hands with myself. Last week it was so hot Daisy was giving evaporated milk!"

"Are you sure it wasn't mastitis?" was my expert reply.

Where do cows go for lunch?

The calf-eteria!

A beef cattle farmer called Pete Clark with over 1000 head of cattle met his new farming neighbour and greeted him with "Hello, I'm Peter Clark and I farm over a thousand head of cattle. Are you the very famous Joshua Wright?"

Joshua replied "Why? What ya heard?"

"Cattle, I just told you didn't I?" was Pete's reply.

The bull and cow were rubbing noses. The eighteen-year-old farm lad was watching them. He looked at his girlfriend and said, "I want to do the same."

"Go on then, please yourself – they are your cattle," was her reply.

The farmer's wife had a rant and a rave at her husband.

"You never take me out, not even on my birthday. You spend all your time with those cattle, early morning milking, feeding calves, late milking, calving cows, silage making and every other farm job besides. That bull of yours annoys me – what do you call him? Romeo is it? He serves at least 50 times a year – why can't you do that?"

"Because the bull doesn't mate with the same old cow every time!" was his cutting reply.

Why did the bull rush?

Because he saw the cowslip.

When buying your first field or farm your solicitor will need to carry out all your legal requirements and you will have stamp duty and legal fees to pay. Don't forget the old farming question, "What's the difference between your bull and your solicitor?"

"The solicitor charges more!"

What has only one horn but gives lots of milk?

The milk tanker.

David, a young farmer, knocked at the door of his neighbouring farmer. Julie, the farmer's daughter, answered the door.

"Hello, David. If you have come to borrow our prize winning Hereford bull to go with your cows my father charges £100, but if you only want the old bull my father just charges £50."

"No, no," replied David. "I've come because your brother Matthew has got my sister pregnant."

"Oh I don't know what Dad charges for him," was her reply.

A man threw some milk across the street, drenching a pedestrian on the other side. He didn't stop at that; he then threw some butter at him and finally some cheese.

The pedestrian, smothered from head to toe, was understandably upset.

"How dairy!" he exclaimed.

Cattle

Two cows talking in a field: The Holstein said, "I was artificially inseminated this morning."

"No!" replied the Ayrshire.

"Yes, straight up, no bull!" replied the Holstein.

• 2 •

Farmers

A farmer talking to another farmer at market:

"My wife went to the doctor's and said, 'I have a small wart which is really embarrassing me.' The doctor's reply was, 'Leave him.'"

A farmer was talking to a feed representative:

"I never forget a name or a face and on the subject of faces I will remember both of yours!"

A farm worker came for an interview on the farm.

The boss said to him, "I hear you come from a large family. Have you got a brother?"

"No, but my sisters have," the man replied.

The farmer gave his wife an inch and now she thinks she's a ruler.

"How are you getting on with your new farm secretary?" asked Jake at market.

"She's the fattest farm secretary I have ever seen. I don't know how to pay her – by the week, month or pound."

The boss was annoyed.

He said to the farm worker, "You have been late for work every morning this week."

"Yes, boss, but I have been slipping away early."

I asked my boss for some advice. "Should I get married boss?"

"I am lucky with my two women. I have a good secretary who takes things down for me and a lovely wife who picks things up for me so the answer is yes."

An old farmer, 93 years old, married an 18-year-old girl. They had a church wedding and a lovely reception. At the reception her parents gave her a new blanket and his relations gave him only a month to live.

"I dropped my jacket in there," said Paddy.

The boss met two men employed by the council who came out with a tanker to empty the farm cess pit. The pit was emptied and then one of the men stood on top of the full tanker. He had got his sleeves rolled up and was fishing about in the mess, right up to his armpits. His mate couldn't figure it out and asked him what on earth he was doing.

"I dropped my jacket in there," said Paddy.

"Why worry," said his mate, "the council will give you a new one."

"I'm not worried about the jacket. It's just that my sandwiches are still in the pocket!"

A farmer went to the dogs' home. "I would like a blind dog for my mother-in-law."

"Don't you mean a guide dog?"

"No, one look at her and it will go for her throat."

A farmer had his credit card stolen. He didn't report it to the bank or the police because the thief was spending less than his wife.

A farmer talking at market:

"My wife left me over a month ago. She said she was just going out to buy some milk but she didn't come back and she hasn't telephoned – it doesn't matter though because the house cow is now in full milk."

A farmer was talking in the pub:

"Last night the peeping Tom who the police have been trying to catch for years called at the mother-in-law's house and asked her to shut the curtains!"

My farm boss asked me, "Did you hear about the posh wedding at the local church?"

"No," I replied.

"The arable farmer with the 5000 acres – you know he has a son, David – David Cornwall-Jones, well, he has married an arable farmer's daughter, Patty Ferguson-Smyth. Apparently it was the first double barrelled shot gun wedding our vicar has performed!"

"I like your new shoes, boss."

"Yes, John, they are rather special. They are tortoiseshell. It took me four hours to walk out of the shop!"

"Morning, Jacob, how are you and how is the wife?"

"I'm alright but the wife keeps putting on weight – she is so fat she has got more rolls than a bakery and when she went whale watching the whales watched her."

Mo, my old farm boss, went to the doctors.

"Doctor, I keep hearing the same song in my head all the time. I can't concentrate on my work, it just keeps going through my head."

"What is this song?"

"It's Tom Jones' 'The Green, Green Grass of Home'. Is it common?"

"Well, it's not unusual!"

An insurance man tried to sell an accident policy to one of my farming neighbours who shall remain nameless because he is not very bright. The insurance man was not getting very far when he asked his final question.

"How would your wife carry on if you died?"

"Well, it would be no concern of mine as long as she behaves herself while I am alive," was my neighbour's reply.

The farmer's wife asked her husband if they could go out for lunch.

"Well, that new restaurant is no good, it closes on a Monday because that's when they do the washing up!"

Two farmers were talking at market:

"I see they have opened the new RSPCA centre in town, it is very modern and spacious".

"It's a good job then because they couldn't swing a cat in the old centre!" replied the other farmer.

My farm boss painted rabbits on his bald head because at a distance they looked like hares.

Two farmers were talking in the pub:"I witnessed five men beating up the mother-in-law."

"Did you help?"

"No, I said five would manage the job!"

A farmer getting drunk in a pub: "Has a lemon got a beak and two legs, barman?"

"No, sir."

"Sorry, I've just squeezed a canary into my gin and tonic!"

A farmer said to me one day, "If I had a pound for every time I thought about the wife, I would start thinking about her today."

The farm workers had a day out to the seaside on a coach – it was a mystery tour. They had a bet on the bus to guess where they were going. The driver won £42.

Our local Lord of the Manor who is also a farmer and large landowner, has a new butler with his left arm missing – it serves him right.

*My farm boss had got a pair of stuffed foxes in the corner of
the kitchen.*

My farm boss had got a pair of stuffed foxes in the corner of the kitchen.

"Do you like the foxes?" he asked. "I shot them this autumn. The taxidermist asked me if I wanted them mounting. 'No,' I said. 'One standing up and one sitting down will do nicely!'"

The farm boss advertised for a worker to come and fell his wood.

A smallish chap came for an interview and the boss said, "Show me what you can do."

He was amazed just watching him. He cut down twenty trees in no time at all.

"Where did you learn to cut trees down that quickly?" asked the farmer.

"The Sahara Forest."

"Don't you mean the Sahara Desert?"

"Well, that's what it's called now!"

A farm worker went into the country store to buy a rat trap.

"Hurry up. I've got a bus to catch."

"Our traps don't catch buses, sir!" was the assistant's reply.

A farmer talking:

"My wife has calves that only a cow would love."

My farm boss always dressed like a farmer, with a cap, checked shirt, brown trousers and boots. Then one day I saw him going out with his wife. He was wearing a very colourful pink and green shirt.

"That shirt is a bit loud, boss."

He was a bit embarrassed but he replied quickly, "I haven't got my muffler on yet."

"My wife always wanted a lovely coat so I bought her a mink outfit – a rifle and four traps," joked a farmer I know well.

I asked a farmer that I knew quite well at market, "How come you are not married?"

"Well, actually I have been married twice. My first wife died of mushroom poisoning. My second wife died of a broken neck."

"Oh, how awful, how did that happen?" I asked.

"She wouldn't eat the mushrooms!" was his reply.

A farmer talking:

"I wouldn't say my wife was old but she had that many candles on her birthday cake it looked like a prairie fire."

The old farmer was sitting in a pub with his wife drinking his pint of bitter.

"I love you," he remarked.

"That's the nicest thing you have said to me in years but is it the beer talking or you?"

"Well, actually I was talking to the beer!"

A local farmer had an accident and drove into a car driven by a dwarf.

"I'm not happy," said the dwarf.

"So who are you?" asked the farmer.

A farmer buys a new pair of boots.

"They feel too tight," he said to the shop assistant.

"Try pulling the tongue out," suggested the assistant.

"No, they thtill feelth too thight!" replied the farmer.

"What are you doing this evening?" asked one farmer to another.

"I'm going to watch my wedding video backwards."

"Why on earth do you want to do that?"

"I really like it when she takes the ring off, walks backwards down the aisle and gets back into the car and is driven out of sight."

My old farming boss never read farming books or magazines, not even the 'Farmer's Weekly'. The great debate of the 1970s was about entry into the Common Market. This was right outside his frame of reference, though he would never admit it.

"Should we join the Common Market?" I asked him one day in an attempt to stimulate a bit of intelligent conversation.

"Well, I don't know." he reflected. "As long as it doesn't clash with Rugby Cattle Market on a Monday or Melton Mowbray Market on a Tuesday or Leicester on a Wednesday then I haven't got any objections."

"I enjoy my evenings. I stretch out on the sofa, drink a lager after a good meal and then watch the wife's favourite programmes on the television!"

I congratulated the old farmer on his wedding anniversary.

"We have been married 49 years and do you know I can't remember breaking 7 mirrors!"

A farmer was standing in one of his fields. An aeroplane loses its load of Datsun car parts which start falling into the field.

"Look, it's raining Datsun cogs!" he shouted.

A farmer parked his car on a car park on the edge of town in a rundown area.

A youth jumped on the bonnet and said "I will look after your car for you – it will only cost you £20."

"No need, son, I've got a Rottweiler in the car so it won't get vandalised or stolen."

"What's the dog like at putting fires out?" was the youth's reply.

The farmer said to his wife, "I was a fool when I married you."

"Yes, but I was in love and didn't notice," replied his wife.

An old farmer was telling me, "When I got married fifty odd years ago I said to my new wife on our wedding night, 'I don't mind you wearing your see-through nightie but I wish you wouldn't wear your vest underneath it!'"

A farmer broke his glasses on a Friday afternoon and quickly went to the opticians. It was too late to get anything done so they boarded them up until Monday.

A farm boss interviewed a young farmer for the job advertised in the paper.

"Can you cut and lay a hedge?"

"No."

"Can you milk cows?"

"No."

"Can you shear sheep?"

"No."

"Can you make tea?"

"Yes."

"Can you drive a fork lift truck?"

"Oh – how big is the teapot?"

Farmers

The farm boss talking to another farmer at market:

"The wife has got sinus problems – she says sinus a cheque for that new outfit, sinus a cheque for my new handbag and it just goes on and on!"

My old farm boss:

"What's the difference between my neighbour, Clive Roberts, and a coconut?"

"I've no idea!"

"You can get a drink out of a coconut."

A farmer from Texas went on an organised agricultural holiday to Australia. He stayed on a lovely farm and on his first day he was shown around.

"This is my wheat field," said the Australian proudly.

"That's a small field back in Texas. My wheat field is twenty times larger," exclaimed the Texan.

"This is my herd of cattle."

"Back in Texas I have twenty times as many cattle and they are much larger." The Texan then spotted some wild kangaroos. "What are those?" he asked.

"They are our grasshoppers," exclaimed the Australian. "Do you have bigger ones than those in Texas?"

A salesman visited a farm but was unable to sell the boss anything.

"How long will it take me to get to Overfield Farm?" he asked.

"It's a ten minute walk away if you run," was the boss's reply.

A farmer talking at market: "I thought we had a great honeymoon. When I got back home I was thrilled and I felt like a new man. Unfortunately the wife said she did too and now she has left me!"

"Last Wednesday I had to visit the mother-in-law. I have yet to receive a good meal there. This time was no exception. I just got cold shoulder and a salty tongue."

"Bob, would you say your wife was pretty?"

"Pretty, no – she spent three hours at the beauticians and that was just for an estimate!"

A farmer talking about his wife: "Most wives would be content with a romantic love story to read or even a thriller but my wife likes the cheque book. She won't put it down until it is finished – she costs me a fortune."

A farmer asks his wife: "What is hanging from the ceiling and is very black and frizzy?"

"I've no idea," she replies.

"That apprentice electrician that turned up this morning to put some new lights in the milking parlour!"

A blonde lady who had dyed her hair brown pulls up in her car and talks to the sheep farmer.

"If I guess how many sheep you have got can I have one?" she asks.

The farmer is a keen gambler and says "Yes".

"Two hundred and fifty one," she says.

The farmer was amazed, it was exactly right.

She picked one out and put it in her car. Just before she drove off the farmer asked, "If I can guess the real colour of your hair can I have my dog back please?"

I asked my farm boss if I could wash my hands.

"Yes – but what is the difference between a bison and a buffalo?"

"I don't know."

"You can't wash your hands in a buffalo."

The farmer said, "I'm not paying income tax to the Inland Revenue because I have sold the farm and bought one by the coast."

Crows were being knocked down on the road near the farm entrance. Scientists carried out a survey and found 90% were knocked down by lorries and only 10% by cars. They came to the conclusion that there was a look out crow that kept watch. After observing him, they realised he could say "cah" but never "lorry"!

• 3 •

Horses

David farmed on Dartmoor. He was out checking his sheep, lost concentration and got stuck in a bog. He managed to use his mobile phone and contacted Big Bill to pull him out. Big Bill arrived and pulled and pulled but couldn't free him so he telephoned for extra help and two more strong men arrived. Now Big Bill, Charlie and Donald pulled hard on the ropes but it was to no avail, they could not free him, he was firmly stuck.

Then David said "I've got an idea, how about if I take my feet out of the stirrups?"

When does a horse talk?
    Whinney wants to.

You can lead a horse to water but a pencil must be lead.

Why don't some horses like going out after dark?
    They get nightmares.

A white horse goes into a bar and orders a whisky.
    The barman says, "We have Bells, Southern Comfort and White Horse so that last one must be named after you."
    "What, Bill?" was the horse's reply.

Horses have never been very good at dancing because they have two left feet.

A fellow is driving too fast and ends up putting his car into the ditch. A farmer appears on the scene with his Shire horse, Dobbin.
    "I can pull you out with Dobbin here for £20."
    The fellow said, "Yes, please, as quick as you can."
    The farmer hitched Dobbin up to the car with a length of strong chain. The farmer then said, "Pull, Dobbin. Now you pull Dolly, old girl," and the car started to move. The farmer then said, "Pull, Captain," and the car was easily pulled out of the ditch.

"Thank you," said the fellow, "but I am confused. Why did you call your horse by three different names?"

"Oh," said the farmer, "Dobbin is blind and if he thought he was the only one pulling he wouldn't pull at all!"

What side of the horse has the most hair?
The outside.

The farmer was worried because his wife had an upset stomach through eating a horse burger and she spent some time in the hospital. She is now in a stable condition.

What animal has more hands than feet?
A horse.

What type of bread did the farmer feed his horse?
Thoroughbred.

Two men drive around the farms looking for somewhere to go shooting. They tried five farms with no luck and were about to give up when they tried one last farm.

"I'll stay in the car this time," said Max. "You go and ask the farmer."

So Joe went and found the farmer.

"My friend and I would like somewhere to shoot rabbits and crows. Can we have permission to shoot here, please?"

"Yes," said the farmer, "but can you do me a favour? My daughter has left home and that old pony of hers is thirty years old and is not well. Would you shoot him for me?"

"Yes, easy," was Joe's reply. He went back to the car and said, "Come on, Max, we can go shooting."

So off they went down the field and immediately Joe went up to the pony and shot it.

"This is fun," said Max, "I'm going to enjoy shooting here." And he went up to a cow and shot it.

What is the difference between the weather and a horse?

The weather rains down and the horse reins up.

A farmer had a lovely horse but he wouldn't go out.

He was a Shire horse.

A farmer's daughter goes to a hotel on Sunday. She stays three nights and leaves on Sunday. How does she do this?

Her horse is called Sunday.

The horses that say neigh are the ones with the negative attitude.

A farmer bought a racehorse. At the racecourse the farmer was grooming him and then slipped something into his mouth. The clerk of the course spotted him and said, "Are you doping that horse? I have just seen you give it something."

"No, sir, it was just a lump of sugar. I will prove it to you." And with that he took a lump of sugar out of his pocket and ate it.

"I think I had better try that," said the clerk of the course, so he was given one which he swallowed.

Just before the race the farmer gave the jockey some advice.

"You should win. Hold the horse back until the last two furlongs and then let him go. Don't worry if anything passes you because it will either be me or the clerk of the course!"

Two horses talking: "Any pal of yours, Dobbin, is a palomino."

What is a horse's favourite sport?
  Stable tennis.

The lad working on a farm was fed up with the job and went for a job at the farriers.
  "Can you shoe horses, lad?" asked the farrier.
  "No, but I can shoo sheep!"

What breed of horse can jump higher that the farm house?
  All breeds because farm houses can't jump at all.

A farmer has got a horse grazing in a field next to the road. A fellow drives up to the farm and says, "That horse looks pretty good. I would like to buy him. I can give you £2000."
  "He doesn't look so good and I don't really want to sell the horse," replied the farmer.

"He does look good and I will pay you £2500."

"I still think he doesn't look so good but you can have him for £2500."

The next day the fellow came back to the farm. "That horse you sold me is blind – I want my money back."

"I told you he didn't look so good!"

A farmer owned a sad horse. The horse had always got a long face.

The horse was so late getting in from the race he tiptoed into the stables.

A farmer and his new bride are riding home in a horse drawn cart. The old horse stumbles and the farmer says, "That's once." The horse stumbles again and the farmer says, "That's twice." He stumbles again and the farmer says, "That's three times!" and he shoots the horse. His wife says, "That's a nasty, mean thing to do!"

The farmer replies, "That's once . . ."

Why did the horse eat noisily and dribble food out of his mouth?
He had no stable manners.

A farmer has two horses but he can't tell them apart. A farmer friend offers some help.

"Try clipping the mane on one of them but not the other."

Sometime later in the year his friend came back.

"Can you tell them apart now?"

"No, the mane grew back!"

"So try clipping the tail," was his next suggestion, which he did. Months later the friend came back to the farm.

"Can you tell them apart now?"

"No, the tail grew back!"

"Well try measuring them. One might be slightly smaller than the other."

Months later the friend came back again. "You were right," said the farmer. "The black one was smaller than the grey one."

Why are most horses fit and well?

Because they are on a stable diet.

A farmer owns a racehorse but sadly the horse hurt his leg in his last race. The farmer calls out the vet.

"Will I be able to race this horse again?" asks the farmer.

"Yes," says the vet, "but if you do you will probably beat him!"

What is the difference between a horse and a duck?
One goes quick and the other goes quack.

The hardest thing about learning to ride is the ground that you fall off onto.

A farmer won the lottery and decided to give away all of his livestock and retire from farming. He went to the small village and gave a horse to the household where the man was the boss and a duck to the household where the lady was the boss.

At the last house at the end of the village he was undecided and didn't know the people very well.

"Who is the boss?" he asked the couple.

"I am," said the man proudly.

"What colour horse do you want, grey or bay?"

"Grey," replied the man.

"No, make it bay," said his wife sternly.

"Here is your duck," said the farmer handing it to the man.

What does it mean if you find four horse shoes?
There's a horse somewhere walking about in his socks.

How long should a horse's legs be?
They must be long enough to reach the ground.

Some horses are so polite that when you are out riding and you come to a fence they will stop and let you go over first.

What do you call a horse that lives next door?
A neigh-bour.

Horse meat has been found in burgers and pies and has been sold as beef. This scandal, of course, made national headlines. However, one leading supermarket representative was quoted as saying, "Our meat is of very high quality and has to clear a number of hurdles before it goes on sale!"

A farmer heard a horse walking down the road but it was only going clip, clip, clip – it was a two legged horse.

*Our local theatre group have a thespian pony –
it is a little horseplay.*

What is a horse called that has won every race that he has ever been entered in?

Sherbet.

A farmer was formerly in the army. He retired from the army and wrote a book called "One Hundred and Fifty Miles on Horseback". His name was Major Bumsore.

A farmer had a milk round and a racehorse. He said to the horse, "If you don't win tomorrow you will be pulling the milk cart."

The next day the horses were lined up for the start of the race and ready to go except for this horse – he was asleep.

The racecourse starter said "Why are you asleep?"

"I'm getting some rest because I will need to get up at three o'clock tomorrow morning!"

A fellow telephones some stables.

"I need to hire a horse for Saturday."

"Try putting a brick under each hoof."

Two horses met and hadn't seen each other for a long time.

One said, "The pace is familiar but I can't remember the mane."

Farmer said to his wife, "I've been riding this morning."

"Horseback?"

"He came back into the yard before I did!"

A stallion and a mare were due to get married but the mare was left at the church – the stallion didn't turn up because he got colt feet!

• 4 •

Arable Farming

Farmer Reg Price sold loose corn until he got the sack.

Why did the apple pay a visit to the doctor?
It wasn't peeling well.

A woman telephoned her husband at work and asked him to buy some organic vegetables on his way home. The husband arrived at the shop and began to look for organic vegetables. He couldn't find any so he finally asked a shop assistant where they were. The assistant didn't know what he was talking about so the husband said, "These vegetables are for my wife, have they been sprayed with poisonous chemicals?"

The assistant replied, "No, you will have to do that yourself."

"Are potato tops poisonous?" I asked Graham.
"Oh yes, Sir. One bite and you've had your chips."

I said to my farm worker, "You're lazy."
"Me lazy?" he replied, "don't get me started."

Why did the plum go out with an old prune?
   He couldn't get a date.

A farmer was combining his wheat on a hot summer afternoon in August. Sadly he ran over a very attractive Essex girl dressed in designer clothes and covered in expensive jewellery. There was so much mess it took the farmer two hours to sort out the wheat from the chav.

What do you call a retired legume?
   A has bean.

What do you call two rows of brassicas?
   A dual cabbage way.

Two potatoes kept falling out because they couldn't see eye to eye.

Clive Straw was a criminal who was visiting farms by night and stealing. Over the course of six months he had stolen three tractors, two telescopic forklifts, a baler and a muck spreader. His final theft was 1000 bales of straw and 1500 bales of hay. He was found guilty at Warwick Crown Court and the headline in the newspaper the next day was simply, "Straw bailed".

Why do potatoes make good detectives?
    They have their eyes peeled.

What is small, whitish, lives in vinegar and laughs?
    A tickled onion.

I taught a lesson on cereals using one or two witticisms to help keep the students' interest.

"Since we are talking about cereals we will have part one this week, part two of the 'cereal' next week and part three the week after!"

The class groaned.

"Well," I continued, "I couldn't think of 'oat' else to say and 'wheat' a minute, there's 'barley' enough time to finish this lesson."

By now the class were squirming.

"I don't know 'rye' I bother telling you lot these 'corny' jokes! I'm simply 'amaized' you don't all laugh."

The following week I asked the class questions on what they had remembered with special reference to the use of the different crops. I asked Richard Keightly, "What is malting?" He went into one of his ceiling pondering routines, grimacing with concentration. Finding no answer on the ceiling he scrutinised the floor but found no solution there either. Then a smile broke out on his face, he positively beamed.

"I'm not exactly sure, Sir. (My heart sank) But I think that malting is what my cat does when it loses its hair," he replied.

The three-year-old farmer's daughter was eating a slug.

"Take it out of your mouth – whatever does it taste like?" asked her mother.

"A worm," was the child's reply.

What is the fastest crop a farmer can grow?
Runner beans.

Farmer Brown was fed up with some 14-year-olds stealing his marrows. He thought things over and came up with a good idea. He wrote out a sign and pinned it on to one of the marrows. On the sign was written in large red letters "One of these marrows has been sprayed with a powerful insecticide". Two days passed and no more marrows had been stolen so Farmer Brown was very pleased. However, on the third day he found another note in the field which read "Two of these marrows have now been sprayed with a powerful insecticide"!

Why did the tomato get embarrassed and start to blush?
Because he saw the salad dressing.

What do you call a pea that's in a bad mood?
Grump-pea.

An English teacher at my old school asked her class of twelve year olds to use the word "beans" in a sentence. The students were quick to put up their hands to respond with some answers.

"Come on Paul, let's hear your sentence."

"My father grows field beans on our farm which are sold in the autumn."

"Very good, Paul. Daisy, can you use a sentence using the word 'beans'?"

"At tea time yesterday my mother gave us beans on toast for our tea."

"Very good, Daisy. Sam your turn."

"All of us in this classroom are human beans."

What did the father tomato say to the baby tomato when they were walking in the country?

"Ketchup!"

If you had five swedes in one hand and five turnips in the other what would you have?

Very big hands.

Last year even David's scarecrow won a prize!

At our local agricultural group every year David Clarke wins all the arable prizes in the farm competitions including best crops of wheat, barley, oats, potatoes, sugar beet and oil seed rape. Many farmers are now not bothering to enter as they know they will get beaten. Last year even David's scarecrow won a prize because he was outstanding in his field!

A towny couple drove up our farm drive and asked for some manure to put on their rhubarb.

"Certainly," I said, "but we put custard on ours!"

What is the strongest crop a farmer can grow?
    Muscle sprouts.

The bank manager visited my neighbour's arable farm.

"How much money do you pay your workers?" he asked.

"Well," replied the farmer, "David has been employed for 10 years, he works 40 hours a week and I pay him £380. Alf has been employed for 5 years and he works 30 hours a week and I pay him £240. Then there is this complete idiot who works 110 hours a week and he takes home £20 a week."

"That's the worker I want to discuss things with," replied the bank manager.

The farmer replied "That's me, I'm the complete idiot!"

What crop could bite you if you are not careful?
    Parsnips.

The arable farmer set up a new business but at the start only took home a small celery.

When I was a lad, large round bales had not been invented and in those days British agriculture was ruled by the Ministry of Agriculture, Fisheries and Food not APHA. When round bales were invented and were started to be used on British farms it was rumoured that the "Ministry" wanted to ban them because they wanted to make sure all the cattle were getting a square meal.

The arable farmer was hopping mad.
    His wife trod on his corn.

What crop is very small, red and white in colour and whispers?

A hoarse radish.

When his Lordship asked his gardener which crops he would grow in the garden next year the gardener's reply was:

"I shall grow potatoes, runner beans, broad beans, peas, carrots, parsnips and onions."

"What about turnips?" asked his Lordship.

"No, I wouldn't bother with turn-ups, I always buy trousers with straight bottoms."

• 5 •

Chickens, Ducks, Geese and Turkeys

When I was a teacher I asked one of my 14-year-old students the following:

"What is a pullet?"

His reply was, "Something you put strawberries in when you are out doing 'Pick your own'."

After leaving school at eighteen I worked on a farm for a year before going to college. My first outing on the farm tractor, a "little grey Fergie", was a disaster. There were animals everywhere in the farm yard but when I reversed the tractor and trailer there was one less cockerel. As soon as I heard the awful squawk I slapped on the anchors but it was too late. The cockerel was as flat as a pancake and the kiss of life was out of the question! There was nothing for it I would just have to come clean to my farm boss.

"Er . . . sorry but I've just . . . erm . . . run over one of your cockerels," I stammered. "I'm willing to replace him though."

The boss smiled an even smile. "Get your trousers off then lad and see what you can do with them there hens!"

Why did the chicken start to cross the road but stopped and sat down in the middle?

She wanted to lay it on the line.

You may be lucky in purchasing your farm or fields complete with farm buildings. I wasn't that lucky. I needed to turn my first field into an agricultural business and so, after clearing the site, I certainly needed buildings. My first agricultural building was a poultry house for 3000 laying hens. I signed for it on the dotted line and was very excited. I now felt that I was farming for real, spending some serious money to hopefully make more serious money. To prove I wasn't just playing at it I needed to register for VAT. I told the previous owner of the building after signing on the dotted line that I dreamt of making a million pounds out of poultry like my farming neighbour.

"Did he achieve that?" he asked.

"No," I replied, "he just dreamt of it!"

When I was nine years old my mother sent me to the butchers to buy a chicken for Sunday lunch. The butcher asked, "Do you want a pullet?"

"No," I said, "just wrap it up and I'll put it in my bike bag."

My wife Sarah and our two children Jonathan and Roseanna often go out for a meal at lunchtime on a Saturday, usually going to the same restaurant. However, one particular Saturday we thought we would try somewhere different. Sadly, we were served a terrible meal, the soup was cold and I complained to the waiter which is something I haven't done before.

"This chicken soup is cold and in fact there is no chicken in it," I said sternly.

"There is no horse in the horse-radish sauce either," was his cutting reply.

If a hen appears to be acting the fool and laughing do you think it's a comedihen?

The farm boss and his wife took over a hundred hens to market and they all sold, making a good price. His wife suggested that they could spend some of their money on a meal in the cafe at the mart and it would save her cooking when they got home. They had a splendid time and then set off on their journey home. Unfortunately, they were stopped by the police because one of their brake lights wasn't working. The boss got into a heated argument with the police officer. Finally his wife could stand it no more and turned to the officer and said, "Take no notice, officer, he's always like this when he's had a few drinks!"

A customer came to buy some eggs off me.

"I'm pleased with these new hens and in fact these are the best eggs I have had for years," I said proudly.

"Can I have some you haven't had for so long?" was his quick reply.

A lady was sitting in a pub with a bottle of champagne. A man came into the room, ordered a bottle of champagne and sat at the next table.

"Are you celebrating?" enquired the lady.

"Yes," the man replied.

"What a coincidence, so am I!" she said. "What are you celebrating?" The man looked very happy. "I am celebrating because I am a poultry farmer and after many years of trying I am at last getting fertile eggs from my hens. What are you celebrating?" he asked.

The lady looked very happy indeed. "I am celebrating because after many years of trying I am finally pregnant. What is your secret?" she asked.

"I have used a different cockerel," the farmer replied.

"What a coincidence – so have I!" the lady replied with a glint in her eye.

How did the frozen chicken cross the road?

In a shopping bag, of course!

One of my lessons at secondary school was to look at the external features of chickens. I brought some into the classroom and the 14-year-old students were asked to look at combs, wattles, feathers and toes.

I asked Angela, "Is the chicken cold or warm to touch?"

"Warm," was the reply.

"What do you think the temperature of the chicken is then Angela?" I asked.

"Do you mean when it has just come out of the freezer or at Gas mark 4?" was her reply.

"Are these eggs fresh?" asked one of my customers loudly and sternly.

"Fresh? Oh yes, in fact they are so fresh the hens haven't missed them yet!" was my reply.

On our way back from holiday in Norfolk we stopped for lunch at a restaurant. Amongst the items on the menu was "smothered chicken". I looked at this twice because smothered chicken is really bad news for me. When our pullets arrive they will sometimes crowd together getting very close to one another and even piling on top of one another in a great bunch consequently they can't breathe and so will smother and suffocate. I once lost 46 birds in one afternoon. I asked the waitress if these chickens on the menu had suffocated perhaps in a corner of a shed! She, of course, had no idea what I was talking about but she did listen. She explained that the chicken on the menu was smothered in sauce, which of course I had realised. She did say she would bring my comments up at the next staff meeting. A year later after returning from holiday again we went back to the same restaurant and, interestingly enough, "smothered chicken" was not on the menu.

The farmer's son, aged nine, was looking forward to his towny cousin coming to stay on the farm for her school holidays. Jenny was seven and soon after she arrived young Peter took her for a guided tour around the farm.

"I'll leave the best 'til last" he kept saying. He showed her the bull, cows, sheep and pigs, keeping her in suspense.

"What is the best?" she finally asked.

"We have got a man eating chicken," was his reply.

She then went very quiet and nervous but he still didn't show her. Finally they went into the house and by this time she was very nervous indeed.

However, there sitting at the table was the farmer eating his chicken dinner!

Why did the chicken cross the school playground?
To get to the other slide.

How do you stop a cockerel crowing on a Monday morning?
Eat him on Sunday!

I have genuinely seen a chicken with four legs – it was only a few days old, the two extra legs were actually smaller than the other two. I asked Dennis the owner, jokingly, if he was going to specialise in breeding four legged chickens.

"I've already started," he replied. "I've got about fifty so far."

"What do they taste like?" I asked.

"I don't know, I haven't managed to catch any yet," was his witty reply.

We had got rats in our chicken shed.

I went to the chemist and asked, "Have you got any rat poison?"

The assistant said, "Have you tried Boots?"

I said, "I want to poison them not kick them to death."

One of my customers for eggs is very careful with his money and will often say my eggs are too expensive; however, he keeps coming and buying them every week. This particular day I had put the price up by ten pence a dozen and so I wasn't looking forward to telling him. He parked his car and then walked into the egg room and put his hand on a stack of eggs. He was obviously suffering from wind because he let out the loudest fart I have ever heard and he didn't say, 'Excuse me'!

Very quickly I said, "If it gives you wind just by touching the eggs you'll probably poo your pants when I tell you the price!"

In the restaurant I said to the waiter, "This chicken has got one leg longer than the other."

The waiter replied, "Do you want to eat it or dance with it?"

Frost in November to carry a duck
The rest of the winter will be sludge and muck.

Note: A frozen pool with ice firm enough to carry the weight of a duck in November is an old saying that means the rest of the winter will be wet and not icy.

Chickens and ducks are, of course, different species and are quite different to keep. Chickens like to be dry and, of course, ducks like to swim. I have kept thousands of chickens and lots of ducks but I have never managed to cross the two. The old story is when a fellow did cross a chicken with a duck the resulting bird walked along the tow path with one foot on the land and one foot in the water crying cockadoodlequack.

What do you call a duck that steals from other ducks?
    A robber duck!

Our cat Henry is a real character and enjoys killing short tailed field voles, mice, shrews, rabbits and even moles. One day he was a real horror and killed and ate one of our ducklings. We now call him the duck filled fatty puss!

Why don't you bring a duck into the toilet?
    It might be a pekin. (A pekin is a breed of duck)

An Aylesbury drake visits Boots.

An Aylesbury drake visits Boots.

"Can I have some lip salve please?"

"Yes," said the assistant, "that will be £1.20, Sir."

"Thank you – put it on my bill please."

Geese are relatively easy to keep. I have kept them in the past both purchasing goslings and breeding them. They make good guard dogs and will make a lot of noise when someone is about. I had a friend years ago who kept a lot of geese – in fact, he was an enthusiast and he talked of little else. He didn't get on very well with his wife but one day he was keen to show me a photograph of her at the back of his watch. He looked at it, sighed and said "Perhaps I will love her in time!"

At a pub quiz one of the questions was, "What is the Latin name for a goose?" Unfortunately no-one could think of the Anser.

A farmer transporting 27 geese and ten turkeys gave a lift to a passing hitch hiker. Unfortunately the land rover and trailer were involved in an accident and the trailer tipped over. The geese were all badly injured and were flopping about, some with broken legs and wings and so he shoots them all. He looked at the turkeys and they were very badly injured and so he shot them as well. Finally the collie dog was in a bad way so he shot him.

"How are you feeling?" he asked the hitch hiker.

"Never felt better," was his quick reply.

What did the English goose say to the African goose?

Uganda?

The turkey is a funny bird
Its head goes bobble, bobble
All he knows is just one word
And that is gobble, gobble.

At the Christmas poultry market a friend of mine was selling his turkeys. He met a recently married couple that he knew or thought he knew and got talking to them. He had a conversation with the fellow first and then turned to the lady.

"What happened to that awful, unintelligent, dozy blonde your husband used to go out with?" he asked.

"I dyed my hair," was her very annoyed reply.

The sage and onion bullet has just been invented. You can shoot the turkey and stuff it at the same time.

Five little turkeys standing by the door
One ran off and then there were four.
Four little turkeys under a tree
One ran off and then there were three.
Three little turkeys with nothing to do
One ran off and then there were two.
Two little turkeys in the midday sun
One ran off and then there was one.
One little turkey had better run away
For here comes the farmer it's Christmas Day.

• 6 •

Farmers' Wives

My farm boss said to me one day, "I've been married 25 years and have only had one argument. It started on our wedding day and it is still going on today."

The farmer's wife found some paper in her husband's jacket pocket. It said on it "Sweetie Sue". She asked her husband what it was and he told her it was the name of a horse that he had a bet on last Saturday.

About a week later she shouts across the room "Your horse telephoned!"

Two farmers talking at market:

"My wife is attending evening classes to make pottery, this is a step in the right direction because the only thing she has made previously is mountains out of mole hills."

"I said to Gerald, take me somewhere expensive so he took me
to the garage and we filled up with diesel."

Two girls were talking at the Young Farmer's meeting:

"I've come to the conclusion that a good husband is like a parking space – the good ones are already taken."

Women have a number of faults which may include talking too much, however, men have only two faults, everything they say and everything they do.

Two women talking at the Farmer's Market:

"I met my husband in a hotel revolving door and I have been going around with him for years."

One of my farming neighbours bought a lovely new lawnmower, it should last his wife for a number of years.

A farmer's wife went to the psychiatrist which was a waste of money for the first part of the session because she spent 40 minutes rearranging his couch.

Farmers' Wives

A farmer's wife who lives near us told me she had been to the doctor's to see what could be done about her varicose veins.

"I'm fed up with them," she told the doctor. "My husband thinks he is clever because he uses me as a road map."

Jill said to her farming husband, "I look fat and I feel really depressed. Can you give me a compliment to cheer me up and make me feel better?"

"You have impeccable eyesight." was his reply.

Jenny and Vicky were talking outside the school gates.

"Our new farming neighbours seem lovely people. He always kisses his wife when he starts work on the farm in the mornings. I said to my husband 'Why don't you do the same?' Do you know what his answer was, Vicky?"

"No."

"'But Jenny, I don't even know the woman!'"

David's wife looked over the hedge at the neighbouring farm which was distant.

She said to her husband, "I've just seen Luke open the car door for a lady so either he's got a new car or a new lady."

"Can you have a go at mending my watch please?" asked the farmer's wife.

"What for, there's a clock on the oven?" was his cutting reply.

"The two best things about my husband are his open wallet and his closed mouth!"

The farmer's wife went into Currys.

"Can someone serve me with a food mixer please?"

"Kenwood?"

"Thank you, where is he?"

"Brian, I want to learn how to drive," stated the farmer's wife.

"Oh, no!" exclaimed her husband Brian.

"Now you're not going to stand in my way are you?" she remarked without thinking.

The wife of a farmer writes to him in prison and tells him she wants to plant some potatoes in the garden and asks when she should plant them. He writes back and tells her not to plant them in the garden as that's where he has buried the money from the building society robbery. Very quickly, ten big fellows turn up and dig over the garden looking for the stolen money – the prison officers had obviously read the letter. They find nothing but the farmer writes back to his wife and says now is the time to plant the potatoes.

Two farmers' wives talking after church on Sunday: "I have the last say in every argument. Anything at all after that said by my husband is the start of a new argument."

"There are three rings of marriage –
engagement ring, wedding ring and suffering," stated the
farmer's wife in the divorce court.

The farmer's wife said, "My husband has spent very little
attention on me this year and for my birthday he gave me a
ring as a present."

"That sounds nice," replied her friend, Ann.

"No, you have only heard half of it. He gave me a ring
from the pub."

Two farmer's wives talking:"My husband said to me that it's
a fact that women talk twice as much as men. I told him that
was because we had to repeat everything twice."

"What was his reply?"

"It was 'What?'"

"My husband keeps me happy – he firstly lets me think I'm
having my own way and secondly he lets me have it."

Delia was a very overweight farmer's wife. She was talking to her sister who was quite slim. "After David's birthday party yesterday half the cake was left over. I know I'm on a diet but when everyone had gone home I finished the lot. David would be furious but he never found out."

"How did you get away with it?"

"I baked another cake and ate half of that one!"

The farmer's wife said:

"I'm fed up with my husband. Do you know he carries a photograph of me and the three children in his wallet which is lovely but he always says when he looks at it, it reminds him where all of his money is going."

"Jim hasn't spoken to me for two days – he says he doesn't want to interrupt me."

Jill, a farmer's wife, comes home from the doctor's.

"The doctor said for a 55 year old lady I had the skin of a 21 year old."

"What did he say about your 55 year old arse?" asked her husband.

"You were not mentioned," was her reply.

"I asked my husband if we could go to the seaside for the day on the train. 'Oh, no,' he said. 'It's sheer hell on the trains these days.' I don't know why he said that because it's only murder on the Orient Express."

A neighbour of mine sadly had a farm fire. She telephoned the fire brigade.

"Come quickly. It's Grange Farm, which is quite isolated."

"How do we get there?" asked the lady on the switch board.

"Don't you have those red things with the sirens on any more?" asked my neighbour in her panic.

A farmer's wife stood right at the end of the farm buildings and shouted across the field.

"I think I've invented the echo," she said to her husband.

"Listen to yourself," was his reply.

"I think I've invented the echo," she said to her husband.

A fire was found to have been started deliberately. Claire, the farmer's wife telephoned the insurance company on the day of the fire.

"Our barn was insured for £30,000 and so we want to be paid out immediately," she reported.

"It's not quite that easy," replied the man from the insurance company. "We firstly assess the value of your barn and provide you with a new one of comparable worth."

"Well, if that's the way you do things you can cancel the policy on my husband immediately!" she replied very sharply.

• 7 •

Genetics

One of my students, Stuart, told me that his Grandad has grown and selected the most enormous pumpkins but they were so big and heavy that lifting them had given him a rupture so now he was specialising in cucumbers instead.

"Has he developed any new strains?" I asked.

What do you call a fish with no eyes?
FSH.

What do you get if you cross the farm cat with a large male mountain gorilla?

A cat that puts you out of the door at night.

What do you get if you cross the farm cat with a canary?
Shredded tweet.

What do you get if you cross a chicken with a guitar?
A chicken that plucks itself.

What do you get if you cross the farm cat with a Pekinese dog?

Pekin tom.

What do you get if you cross a cow with a turtle?

Turtle neck Jersey.

What do you get if you cross a chicken with a bell?

A chicken that can wring its own neck.

What do you get if you cross a chicken with a cement mixer?

A brick layer.

What do you get if you cross a cockerel with a waitress?

A chicken that lays tables.

What do you get if you cross a sheep with a kangaroo?
   A woolly jumper.

What do you get if you cross an owl with a goat?
   Hootenanny.

What do you get if you cross a parrot with a pig?
   A bird that hogs the conversation.

What do you get if you cross a pig with a conifer?
   Porky-pine.

What do you get if you cross a potato with an onion?
   A potato with watery eyes.

What do you get if you cross an enormous snake with a porcupine?

A roll of barbed wire.

What do you get if you cross a bloodhound with a Labrador?

A blabrador – a dog that keeps barking and barking.

What do you get if you cross a pit bull with a Lassie type dog?

A dog that will bite your head off and then run for help.

What do you get if you cross a sheep dog with a bunch of roses?

A collie flower.

What do you get if you cross a telephone with a golden retriever?

A golden receiver.

What do you get if you cross a farm dog with a tiger?
A postman who is absolutely terrified.

What do you get if you cross a sheepdog with a jelly?
Colliewobbles.

What do you get if you cross a dog with a cockerel?
A poodle that cocks its own doodle.

What do you get if you cross a sheep with a border collie?
A sheep that rounds itself up.

What do you get if you cross the little farm dog with a vegetable?
A Jack Brussel.

What do you get if you cross a dog with a blind mole?
A dog that keeps barking up the wrong tree.

What do you get if you cross a chilli pepper, a shovel and a terrier?

A hot diggity dog.

What do you get if you cross a Rottweiler with a Labrador?

A dog that bites you and then runs off with the toilet roll.

What do you get if you cross a computer with a Rottweiler?

A computer with lots of bites.

What do you get if you cross a collie with a cheetah?

An animal that chases cars and catches them.

What do you get if you cross a turkey with an octopus?

We would all get to eat a leg at Christmas.

What do you get if you cross a bridge with a tractor?
To the other side.

The formula for water is H_2O but when it passes through the farm dog it becomes K9P.

• 8 •

Vets

A dairy farmer called the vet because he was very concerned about one of his cows. The vet came out to the farm.

"I'm not happy with this cow she holds her tail up or to one side all the time and if you look closely it looks as if she has got a lettuce growing out of her backside."

The vet took hold of the cow's tail and took a long look. "I can just see a leaf," remarked the vet.

The farmer replied, "I suppose that's just the tip of the iceberg!"

The vet examined a ewe and turned to the shepherd and said, "I'm sorry your ewe has got blue tongue."

"I didn't even know my sheep had got mobile phones!" remarked the shepherd.

"I'm not happy with this cow she holds her tail up or to one side all the time and if you look closely it looks as if she has got a lettuce growing out of her backside."

*The farmer's dog swallowed a bullet. "What shall I do?" he
asked the vet.
"Be careful and don't point him at anybody."*

A farm student telephoned the vets, "I think my Rottweiler has been killed by my neighbour's Chihuahua."

"Impossible," said the vet.

"No, the Rottweiler got the Chihuahua stuck in his throat."

These days if disease breaks out we have movement records so APHA can see exactly where livestock have been moved to and from. There are also rules on transporting livestock and the animals' welfare is very important. Vets are, of course, highly skilled people and I was told by a vet that the difference between bird flu and swine flu is that for bird flu you need tweetment and for swine flu you need oinkment.

A client takes his dog to the vets. "He's swallowed a roll of film."

"Let's hope nothing develops!" was the vet's reply.

The vet said "This bull needs treatment fast; I'm going to give him steroids."

The stockman looked puzzled, he pulled a face and thought for a while. "I thought they were things you put on the stairs to stop the carpet moving about."

The vet gave the farmer some ointment to rub on the sow which had come out in spots. "Will this cure her?" asked the farmer.

"I never make rash promises," replied the vet.

The veterinary lecturer asked one of his farm students, "What is a caesarean section?"

"A district in Rome," was the student's reply.

The shepherd takes an old ewe to the vets. The vet looked at it and said "I'm afraid the ewe is dead."

"I don't believe it – I want a second opinion," was the shepherds reply.

With that a cat walked into the surgery, sniffed the old ewe and meowed.

"There you are – the cat agrees with me," remarked the vet.

"I still don't believe it – I want another opinion."

With that a Golden Labrador walked into the surgery. He sniffed the old ewe and barked.

"There you are – now the dog agrees with me. She is definitely dead. That will be £250 please."

"What! £250 just to tell me the ewe is dead – that's outrageous!" remarked the annoyed shepherd.

"No, don't forget that as well as my examination you have had a cat scan and a lab report," was the vet's reply.

The farmer telephoned the vet.

"I dropped my money in the pig pen and the sow's eaten it. She has got terrible stomach ache."

"Leave her for now and we will see if there is any change in the morning," instructed the vet.

The shepherd takes his faithful collie to the vets with an ear infection. The vet examined the dog and picked him up.

"I'm sorry I'm going to have to put the dog down," said the vet.

"What – just for an ear infection?"

"No – because he is too heavy!"

Vets

The old farmer telephoned the vets.

"My sow has swallowed my best fountain pen. What is the best thing to do?"

"Try using a pencil until I can pay a visit."

A farmer went to the vets with his Labrador.

"The dog has hurt his leg in several places," he told the vet.

"Don't take him to those places anymore," instructed the vet.

The cowman got the cows in for milking as usual and while he was getting them in he noticed something very unusual. It was a cow which looked as if she had a strawberry growing out of her head. He took a good look at it and he had certainly never seen anything like it before so he quickly telephoned the vet. The vet was quick to come out on to the farm and he examined the cow.

The cowman said "What shall we do?"

"I'll give you some cream to put on it," replied the vet.

A farm student walks into the vet's surgery with a small dog under his arm.

"I want you to help me out," he said.

"Which way did you come in?" asked the vet.

A farmer's daughter called the vet out to see her pony.

"I think he has got a sore throat," she said.

"I just think he is a little hoarse," replied the vet.

The wise old lecturer at veterinary college had worked with thousands of veterinary students over the years. His first year students gathered around the front of the room to watch his demonstration on their first day. He took a white sheet off a dead cow revealing it to the class.

"There are two basic rules you must learn today if you want to be a vet. Number one, don't be disgusted at any part of any animal. Let me show you."

With that he stuck his finger up the cow's nose and quickly put his finger in his mouth and sucked it.

"Now you do it" he instructed the class. Some were hesitant, many pulled faces but each student eventually completed the task.

"Now the second basic rule is observation. If you had watched me closely you would have seen that I put my middle finger up the cow's nose and sucked my index finger!"

The farm cat had been to the vets. Two female cats were talking.

"I would like a night out with him," remarked one cat.

"Oh, you are wasting your time," said the other cat. "He talks about his operation all the time."

"Now then, veterinary. Those injections I have been giving my sow – she seems a bit better but she tends to flush a lot."

"Don't worry about her, it's just a chain reaction."

A vet and a surgeon joined forces, working closely together on a unique project. One of the doctor's patients had lost an ear in an accident. The vet obtained a pig's ear, reshaped it and the surgeon did a marvellous job sewing it onto his patient's head. However, after a few weeks the patient returned and complained to the surgeon that he could hear unusual noises in his new ear. The surgeon examined him but couldn't explain so he then went to ask the vet's advice.

The vet examined him and said, "There is nothing to worry about. It's just a bit of crackling."

Pigs

What's the difference between a pork chop and pea soup?
Anyone can chop pork.

Really cold hard winters make life difficult on a farm. It's hard work walking about in a foot of snow and it is no fun when the water pipes freeze and you have got to go out and thaw them out. The best part of the day is when you have finished work and are back in the warm. My old farm boss looked at his sow and was concerned that she was very cold.

He said to his wife, "I think I will have to bring her inside the house."

"But it stinks," replied his wife.

"The pig will get used to it," replied Mo.

*"Well, what **is** she doing?"* roared Mo.

My old farm boss Mo used to tell the tale of moving a pig before "all these fancy regulations", as he put it, came into force. He had a sow which lived in the orchard at the front of the farm house. He had just got married but no honeymoon or fancy hotel for him and his new bride, it was a quick wedding, a small reception and then back to the farm. He did say that he could lie in bed as a treat as he hadn't had a lie in for 15 years. However, they could only lie in bed if his sow was just lying down and not rolling in the mud. If she was rolling in the mud she would be on heat and would need taking to the farm next door in the wheelbarrow. So they went to bed and the next morning Mo told his new wife to get out of bed and look through the window.

"Is she rolling in the mud or just lying down?" he asked.

"Rolling in the mud," was her reply.

Mo got up and dressed and put the sow in the wheelbarrow to take her next door to Bill's large white boar. The sow was served and Mo returned with her. He told his wife they would get their lie in bed tomorrow. Tomorrow came and again Mo sent his wife to look through the bedroom window.

"Is she rolling in the mud or just lying down?" he asked.

"Rolling in the mud," was her reply.

"I'll take her next door again, we won't get our lie in but it's good stockmanship to have her served twice."

Again he got up, got dressed and put the sow in the wheelbarrow. He took her to Bill's boar and again the sow was served.

On the third morning Mo said, "I am confident we can have our lie in bed this morning. Go on girl, get out of bed and have a look out of the window. She should be lying down – is she?" he asked.

His wife was silent.

"Well, is she rolling in the mud?"

At last his new wife replied, "No, she's not lying down and she's not rolling in the mud."

"Well, what *is* she doing?" roared Mo.

"Sitting in the wheelbarrow," was her reply.

Note: A sow rolling in the mud is not necessarily on heat!

What do you call a pig that enjoys karate as a hobby?

A pork chop.

My wife Sarah, our two children Jonathan and Roseanna and I often go out for lunch on a Saturday. Sausage and egg is on the menu and I often think to myself that it is just a day's work for the hen but a life time commitment for the pig. It is a poor restaurant really, when I asked to speak to the manager the waitress told me he had gone out for lunch.

My first pig was called Ink because he kept running out of his pen.

Two pigs went to a party. They got boared and went home.

A man is driving his brand new Jaguar quite fast along a very winding country lane near our farm.

A lady driver passes in the opposite direction and shouts, "Pig!"

He instinctively sees red and shouts back, "Bitch!"

The man drives around the very next bend and crashes his car into a pig.

A farmer was talking at market.

"David my neighbouring pig farmer was the best friend I could ever have. I could always borrow farm equipment from him or borrow his boar. However, he has run off with my wife and I do miss him."

A farmer was telling his friend about his life.

"Before I was married I was just a simple pig farmer with no buttons on my shirt and look at me now – I have no shirt."

A farm salesman selling animal feedstuffs visited a farm in Leicestershire. After selling some feed to the farmer he looked at the pigs. They were all free range and looked well eating his brand of pig feed. However, he did notice that one pig had got three legs.

"Why has that pig got only three legs?" he asked the farmer.

"Well I must tell you," said the farmer excitedly. "I was underneath the tractor replacing parts and I trapped myself somehow between the wheel and the mudguard. I couldn't get free. I shouted and shouted but no one heard me and of course I hadn't got my mobile phone. I was well and truly stuck but I seemed to be uninjured except for some bruises. That pig saw me and he knew I was in trouble so he ran all the way up to the house and fetched my wife, she found me and then she fetched help. I was finally safe."

"I understand this," replied the salesman, "but it doesn't explain why he has only got three legs."

"Well, if you have a pig as good as that you can't eat him all at once can you?"

What do you call a pig that has laryngitis?
Disgruntled.

A towny school teacher from Birmingham took her class on a farm visit. They had a wonderful day looking at all the farm animals and had a lovely picnic in the orchard. At the farm the children had to fill in a work sheet answering questions about the animals. The next day at school the teacher went through the answers.

"Jenny – why did the chickens have to be shut in their pen at night?"

"To stop the fox killing them, Miss."

"Correct. Peter – why did the sheep have so much wool?"

"To keep them warm, Miss."

"Correct. Amy – why have the cows got udders?"

"To store the milk, Miss."

"Correct. Eric – why was the pig so fat?"

"Because twelve piglets lay next to her blowing her up, Miss!"

Our neighbouring pig farmers recently gave a party. It was a cheese and swine party.

A farming couple I know very well have been married for 50 years. Mavis suggested to Harry that they should have a party on the farm in the form of a barbeque.

"We could kill a pig," said Mavis excitedly.

"That's not fair at all," remarked Harry. "Why should the pig take the blame for something that happened 50 years ago?"

The farmer was upset because the solicitor's dog ate £10 worth of fresh pork out of his Land Rover. After much arguing the solicitor agreed to pay £10 but two weeks later the farmer received a bill for £140 for the solicitor's time and consultation fee!

Many years ago an unpopular Prime Minister was being chauffeured in a top of the range Jaguar and he was meant to be going to an important meeting. Sadly they ran over a pig; it was just outside a farm drive in a country lane. The chauffeur went to the farm to admit what he had done. He left the Prime Minister in the car and knocked on the door of the farm house. He was asked in and the door was shut. The Prime Minister waited patiently at first but then he kept looking at his watch as time ticked by and the chauffeur still did not appear. Finally almost two hours later the chauffeur came back to the car.

"Where have you been?" asked the Prime Minister sternly.

"Well it was great; they gave me a wonderful meal and £200."

"Why?"

"I told the farmer I was the Prime Minister's chauffeur and I just killed the pig."

What do you call a pig that steals?
    A hamburglar.

The farmer and his wife decided to diversify from farming and started to take in paying guests.

"Did you sleep well?" the farmer asked the city gent who was staying.

"Yes, except an old sow kept pushing at the door in the middle of the night."

"Oh, don't worry about that – when we rent out her room she always gets annoyed."

A new neighbour said to me, "When I got married they told me my new wife, Betty, wasn't fit to live with pigs, but I say she is!"

Livestock at our local agricultural show win rosettes, cups and prize money. However, for a change this year the champion pig received a pork medallion.

Farmers' Sons

The farmer was showing his son how to do the farm accounts but his son was struggling.

"Let me give you an example," said his father. "If I've got £10 in this pocket and £20 in this pocket what have I got?"

"Someone else's trousers," was his son's reply.

The farmer retired and handed the farm over to his son and the advice he gave when giving his retirement speech was:

"If you work hard on this farm son, starting work at 6am and finishing work at 9pm you should make a fortune . . . if you strike oil!"

A farmer was talking about his son at market:

"He just doesn't see anything. He doesn't spot a sheep with foot rot or a cow with mastitis; in fact I would go as far as to say he couldn't find an elephant with diarrhoea in the snow!"

The farmer's son was getting married.

"I have got some advice for you son. A woman marries a man expecting he will change but he doesn't. A man marries a woman expecting that she won't change but she does!"

A farmer's son was caught and prosecuted for a series of robberies and was sent to Crown Court.

"Have you anything to say before I pronounce sentence?" asked the judge.

"Sod all, your Honour."

The judge turned to the solicitor and said "What did he say?"

"Sod all, your Honour."

"Well, I could have sworn I saw his lips move!"

"Son, a farmer is someone who will pay £2 for an item in a shop that's £1 just to get done and out of the shop and back to the farm. The farmer's wife will pay £1 for a £2 item she doesn't want because she thinks it's a bargain."

"Dad, I want to become a vegetarian."

"But son, we are beef farmers so I think it will be a huge missed steak!"

A farmer's son started work in the laboratory at a large fertiliser company. However, Rodney is no more because what he thought was H_2O was H_2SO_4!

Note: H_2SO_4 is sulphuric acid.

"What is married life like, Dad?" asked the farmer's son.

His father replied, "Getting married is like going to a restaurant with a friend. You order what you want then you see what your friend had got and you wish you had ordered that!"

"Dad, I'm not working today – it's too hot to do the work that was too cold to do in the winter."

A farmer's son hated farming and so left home and went to the city to get a job as a shoe shiner.

A farmer's son hated farming and so left home and went to the city to get a job as a shoe shiner. He worked on the street cleaning business men's shoes. Now his father makes hay while the son shines.

"I've noticed married women seem to be fatter than single women," observed the farmer's son. "Is that correct, Dad?"

"Yes, son. Single women look in the fridge to see what's there and eagerly go to bed with their boyfriend. Married women look in the bed and see what's there and eagerly go to the fridge."

"I've got a question to ask you before you get married son. If your wife is bawling and shouting at the locked front door and your border collie is barking to be let in at the back door – who do you let in first?"

"I don't know, Dad."

"The dog, because he will quieten down after you let him in the house."

A farmer's son didn't like farming so he joined the army. He came home on leave for the first time and his family were pleased to see him.

"What's the best part about the army, son?" asked his father.

"They let you lie in bed until ever so late in a morning, Dad."

A farmer's son became a punk rocker and with his mate the two of them were in town. One was drinking battery acid and the other one was chewing fireworks. The police charged one and let the other one off.

Rodney took some time off from his farm work to go to the doctor's but the doctor said, "I can't diagnose your problem. I think it's drink."

"I'll come back tomorrow when you are sober, Doctor," was Rodney's reply.

"Dad, I think I have found a girlfriend just like my mother," said the farmer's son.

"All I can give you, son, is sympathy," his father replied.

"I'm not making much money farming but I'm happy. I wish my son was interested. He left the farm and became a dentist. He makes a tremendous amount of money but he is not a happy man. Ever since he married Jenny the manicurist they are always fighting tooth and nail!"

Joe went into the fish and chip shop after a hard day's work on the farm.

"Fish and chips, please."

"The chips are cooked, the fish won't be long."

"It had better be fat then!" was his reply.

"Son, a farmer's wife is someone special. She can spot a blonde hair on your lapel at 4 o'clock in the morning across a darkened bedroom, half asleep but she can't see both the garage doors with the headlights on!"

"That son of mine has it all. He will inherit a large farm, machinery and livestock. In fact he was born with a silver spoon in his mouth and he hasn't even stirred. He is that thick he stayed up all night studying for a blood test!"

"Son, what is the difference between a new wife and a new farm dog?"
"I don't know, Dad."
"After a year the farm dog is still excited to see you."

"Money talks, son, but it doesn't say when it will come back to you!"

"Fetch some nails from the country store, son, please."

He arrives at the store.

"I would like some nails, please."

"How long do you want them?"

"Oh, I want to keep them for good!"

"The farmer's son filled out a job application form and at the bottom where it said 'Sign here' he put 'Taurus'."

"Dad, in some parts of the world a farmer doesn't know his wife until he has married her."

"This happens in every country, son!"

A farmer had four sons – three very tall with dark brown hair and brown eyes and one son who was short with red hair and blue eyes. The old boy was dying and he asked his wife if the last son was his.

"Yes, definitely," was her reply. The farmer was so pleased. After his death she was relieved that he hadn't asked her about the other three!

A farmer's son went to the neighbour's farm.

"Can I borrow your tractor please?" he asked.

"Yes, as long as you don't take it off this farm," was the short reply.

A farmer's son, aged 18, was carrying out ground works for my new bungalow along with a 70-year-old labourer. The young man made fun of the "old boy" and kept on saying he wasn't strong enough to do the work anymore. The wise old boy said, "I can wheel something in the wheelbarrow over to that poultry shed and you won't be able to wheel it back, I bet you £20."

"You're on," said the youth.

The old boy fetched the barrow and said, "Get in son!"

"Dad I'm fed up with working long hours – I want a 40 hour week."

"If I do that I will have to call you Robinson Crusoe, because all of his work was done by Friday!"

• 11 •

Dogs

A sales representative selling animal feed parked his car in the farm yard and as he walked towards the house he noticed an old Border Collie dog just lying in the yard. The dog didn't get up to greet him but remained still. He looked at least fifteen years old. Pinned on his kennel was a note which read "Beware of the dog". After meeting the farmer, the sales rep said, "Why the sign 'Beware of the dog'? That dog is too old to hurt anybody."

"No, he won't hurt anybody – I'm fed up with people tripping over him so I put up the sign," was the farmer's reply.

A farmer owns a dog that has ears and eyes but no nose.

"How does he smell?" asked a neighbour.

"Terrible!"

The farmer's Border Collie went to the flea circus – he enjoyed the performance but at the end stole the show.

Dogs

Why is the heart of the tree like the tail of the dog?
They are both furthest away from the bark.

The farmer's wife was fed up with the dog in the house.
She said to her husband "I'm going to call him Egypt because he leaves pyramids all over the house."

The blind farmer was asked to skydive and raise money for charity but he refused to do it because he said it would scare his guide dog.

What's worse than raining cats and dogs?
Hailing taxis.

"This collie dog chases anyone on a bike," exclaimed the farmer.
"What are you going to do then? This could be dangerous," asked his wife.
"That's easy. I'll take his bike away!"

The barman said, "You can't leave that lyin' there."

A farmer walked into a bar with his dog. He ordered a pint of bitter and then a pint for the dog. They kept drinking and consumed eight pints each. The farmer didn't feel drunk but the dog became drunk and then passed out. The farmer said goodbye to the barman and started to walk towards the door leaving the dog stretched out on the floor.

The barman said, "You can't leave that lyin' there."

The farmer said, "It's not a lion, it's a dog!"

The Lord and Lady at the big manor house were farmers and big landowners but financially they were struggling and needed to make cutbacks. They sacked the maid. The maid was very upset and on hearing the news she took a big juicy rump steak out of the fridge and gave it to the dog. The dog loved it, ate every bit and licked his lips.

"What did you do that for?" asked Her Ladyship.

"That dog has been a great help to me. He always cleans the dishes after supper for me!"

A farmer bought a new dog but after a few days telephoned the original owners.

"I'm not happy because every time a bell rings he goes and sits in the corner."

"Well, he is a Boxer!" was the reply.

A dog has an owner – cats have staff.

Why did the dog keep running in circles, chasing his own tail?

He wanted to make both ends meet.

Two fleas were talking:

"Shall we walk into town or should we take the scruffy old farm dog?"

What did the hungry Dalmatian say after he ate an excellent meal and was full up?

"That hit the spots!"

A farmer's son saw an advertisement for a talking Labrador. He couldn't believe it so he went along to see. He introduced himself at the house and then went into the back garden to meet the dog.

"I'm the only talking dog in the world," said the dog. "I've had a wonderful career based at Downing Street, I helped the government for about five years and actually became a spy which was ideal because no one would expect a dog to listen and then report back what he had heard. I then spent two years at Heathrow airport unearthing crime and drug smugglers. I am a father, fathering over thirty puppies and many of those are show dogs. I now want to retire!"

"Wow!" exclaimed the farmer's son. "How much do you want for this amazing dog?"

"Only five pounds," replied the owner.

"What? Only five pounds. Surely he is worth a lot more money than that! After all he has done in his life!"

"No – he's a liar. He's not done any of the things he has just told you!"

The farmer came into the house.

"I'm shattered. I spent the evening watering my vegetables and that old collie dog of mine never lifted a leg to help me!"

What happens when it rains cats and dogs?

You might have to step in a poodle.

A farmer called his dog Tax because when the dog is outside the back door the farmer says, "Income Tax".

What dog uses the farm telephone?
Dial-matian.

A farmer has had enough of working so he takes the afternoon off and drives to the park to get away from it all, where hopefully it will be stress free. He walks around, feeds the ducks with some bread and then steps in a pile of dog mess. He stops to wipe his shoe on the grass and at the same time sees a woman step into the same pile of mess.

"I just did that!" exclaimed the farmer.

The lady then grabs him by his shirt collar and rubs his nose in it.

What makes more noise than a dog barking outside your window?
Two dogs barking outside your window.

When is a black dog not a black dog?
When it is a greyhound.

The rancher's dog walks into the sheriff's office and says,
  "I'm looking for the guy that shot my paw."

A farmer talking about his wife's sister:
  "She's as ugly as a bulldog chewing a wasp."

The new postman visits the farm for the first time. He's a bit nervous as he walks across the farmyard because he sees a boy with a Rottweiler which isn't on a lead. It was the farmer's son.

  "Does your dog bite, lad?" asked the postman.

  "No, sir."

  "That's good, I'm happier now," answered the postman. With that the dog growled and bit him hard on the leg.

  "You said your dog wouldn't bite!" he said, nursing his wounded leg.

  "This isn't my dog sir," the boy replied.

It's alright if it rains cats and dogs but not if it rein-deer.

The farmer's daughter's collie dog wouldn't round up sheep and was so stupid it only chased parked cars.

The farmer's wife's dog loves to take a bubble bath – it's a shampoodle.

A bitch gave birth to puppies at the side of the road. The puppies were all fine but she got prosecuted for littering.

A Labrador goes into the corner shop to do some shopping every Friday morning. His owner gives him a basket, a shopping list and a purse containing money. He goes up to the counter and wags his tail. The shop owner takes out the list, places the items in the basket and takes out the correct money and the dog walks home with the groceries. This goes on for nearly a year. The grocer is so impressed he follows the dog home with the intention of buying him but when the dog gets to the door of the house he is beaten with a stick by a woman.

"Stop, stop!" shouts the grocer. "He's a good, intelligent dog, what are you doing that for?"

"He's not intelligent, he's hopeless. That's the fourth time he has lost his keys this month," replies the woman.

A newly married farmer takes his dog to the vets.

"Cut his tail off, please, because the mother-in-law is visiting on Saturday and I don't want her to feel the least bit welcome!"

The farmer's daughter called her dog Blacksmith because whenever he wanted to go to the toilet he would make a bolt for the door.

A watchdog will not only look after your property but he will also keep the best time.

What's black and white and very red?

A very embarrassed Dalmatian.

The farmer had got two dogs – a fierce German Shepherd that was the guard dog and a Border Collie who was a working dog. Neither liked to be petted. His six children kept asking for a dog of their own. They asked for birthdays and Christmases and eventually the farmer agreed to buy them a dog. After a great deal of thought, he bought them a lovely dachshund – a dog which they could all pet at the same time.

A dog ate nothing but garlic. His bark was worse than his bite.

A farmer had one of the biggest dogs you've ever seen. He took him to the seaside. He had a Great Dane out.

What has four legs and an arm?
  A very happy Pitbull.

Dogs

A farmer bought a lovely Border Collie puppy. He was very pleased with her on the first day but when the family got up the next morning there was some dog mess at the top of the stairs.

"I'll house train her," said the farmer confidently, and with that he rubbed her nose in the mess and pushed her down the stairs. The same thing happened the next morning, and the next and the next.

"You will never house train that dog," remarked his wife.

"I will," he said even more confidently this time.

The next morning they got up and found the dog had rubbed her own nose in the mess and tumbled to the bottom of the stairs.

Tractors

What did the little blue tractor say to the great big green tractor?

"Park closer to me, John Deere."

The farmer wasn't pleased with his brand new tractor. He was convinced it was dangerous so he took it back to the dealership. The mechanic checked it over and on his written report just put the following:

"The most dangerous part of this new tractor is the nut that holds the steering wheel."

A magic tractor was driven down the lane and turned into a field.

The tractor driver drove the tractor into the field but got well and truly stuck – it was a magnetic field!

The driver of the car said, "I don't know where you find the time to do your farm work, you must do it at night."

A couple were driving down a country lane when the road disappeared under a sea of mud and they got well and truly stuck. A farmer immediately appeared with a tractor and offered to pull them out for £50. They had to agree so the farmer attached a chain to the tractor and pulled their car out of the mud. The farmer remarked that theirs was the twentieth car he had pulled out of the mud that day.

The driver of the car said, "I don't know where you find the time to do your farm work, you must do it at night."

"No," replied the farmer, "that's when I add more water to the mud!"

The farmer's wife was talking to her friend about her husband.

"I'm fed up with him," she remarked. "I can't get him started in the morning. He produces waste gases and doesn't want to work."

"Mm, we've got a tractor like that," replied her friend.

"You're back already – you've never taken the tractor for a service in that time," remarked the farmer.

The farmer instructed his employee to take the tractor for a service. An hour later the worker returned with the tractor.

"You're back already – you've never taken the tractor for a service in that time," remarked the farmer.

"No, I'm back because I couldn't get the tractor up the chapel steps," was his reply.

While riding his bike the vicar came across a tractor and trailer but unfortunately the entire load of bales had fallen off the trailer. A young farmer was working frantically loading the bales back on to the trailer with sweat pouring off him.

The vicar looked at him and said, "Have a rest my son, sit down with me and share my lemonade."

"No," replied the young man, "my father wouldn't like it" and he continued throwing the bales onto the trailer.

"Have a rest, you'll kill yourself," said the vicar more sternly this time.

"No, my father wouldn't let me".

"This father of yours is a slave driver – I'll tell him when I see him. Where is he?"

"He's under the rest of these bales!"

Which tractor comes in a box?
A Case.

Richard, a farmer I know, loves his New Holland tractor and takes a great deal of pride in looking after it and keeping it really smart. I overheard another farmer talking to him at market and I was surprised to hear this fellow say "Did I see your wife driving your tractor last Saturday?"

"No chance whatsoever," was Richard's reply. "She only drives the car from the back seat."

The tractor is often the farmer's pride and joy and many would prefer this to a new car. The teacher in our local primary school recently took a group of seven-year-olds on a farm visit. The next day she asked the class "What noises did we hear on the farm yesterday?"

The replies were "Moo", "Baa", "Oink", "Cockadoodle doo" and "Get off that ******* tractor!"

The young farmer's girlfriend decided to finish the relationship, she didn't tell him, she just sent him a John Deere letter.

A friend of mine was a real tractor enthusiast – all he talked about was tractors. He was a real expert and owned a number of vintage tractors. He collected many scale models from Fordsons to Massey Fergusons and he had a library of tractor books. The walls in his house were covered in tractor posters and framed photographs and paintings of tractors. I was very surprised indeed when he told me he had advertised everything and in fact has sold everything. He now tells me he is an ex tractor fan.

Where did the farmer find his tractor with no rear wheels?
In exactly the same place he left it.

There are not many programmes on television about tractors, in fact they are very few and far between. There is a film, however, called "Tractors". I haven't seen it but I have seen the trailer which looks very good. I believe a panel of judges are getting together to start a new entertaining programme called the X tractor.

What has four fingers and a thumb and drives a tractor?
A farm hand.

Modern tractors today have satellite navigation systems and almost as many controls as an aeroplane. CD players are a must but I remember when stereos were first installed in motor cars. I asked my farm boss if he had got a stereo in his new car. "No," he replied, "I've got the wife in the front seat and the mother-in-law in the back."

Massey Ferguson stands behind all their tractors and implements – except the manure spreaders.

• 13 •

Sheep

Mary had a little lamb
She also had a bear.
I've often seen her little lamb
But I've never seen her bare.

I returned to the school farm one evening to see if any of the ewes were lambing. I was on my own at first but was soon joined by Ian, the caretaker's son, aged four.

"Can I help, Mr Terry?" he asked.

"Yes, if you are a good lad and don't make any noise," I said with a smile. I did not expect any ewes to be lambing as it happened. I had left them over an hour before and all was quiet. I knew his mother was not keen on him watching a lambing but I did not want to hurt his feelings. He could help by giving the ewes a few cabbage leaves. Our sheep like greenstuffs and he would enjoy feeding them.

When I walked into the sheep pen, though, I found a ewe in some difficulty. I immediately slipped off my jacket and pullover, rolled up my sleeves and got down to work. The ewe was straining and when I looked I could see that the head of the lamb was out but no legs. They were both back. Using lubrication I pushed the lamb back into the womb when the ewe was not straining. Out of the corner of

A farmer came to buy some sheep from me.
"I like this ewe but its legs are too short," he said firmly.
"They all reach the floor, don't they?" I replied confidently.

my eye I suddenly became aware of Ian. He was sitting on a bale sucking on a piece of straw and watching me intently. I was worried about letting him stay there but just did not have the time to take him back home – things were too far advanced. I continued pushing the lamb back into the womb and managed to locate the front legs. I straightened them carefully and brought the forelegs and head into the normal presentation position. The lamb was born and I was feeling pleased with myself. Upon closer inspection I realised that my relief had been premature, the lamb looked to be dead. I grabbed it by the back legs, shook it roughly and smacked it. Success! It spluttered and started to breath.

A voice came from behind me, "It serves the little beggar right for crawling up there in the first place!"

Adam, my accountant, came out to the farm to see me to go through the books.

"How are you?" I asked.

"Quite good, thank you, but I can't get to sleep at night very easily," he replied.

"Have you tried counting sheep?" I asked.

"Yes, that's my problem. I make a mistake and then I am awake for three hours trying to find it."

What do you call a sheep that is covered from head to toe in chocolate?

A chocolate baa!

Mary had a little lamb
She tied it to a pylon
Ten thousand volts shot up its tail
And turned its wool to nylon.

Sheep

Most farmers hate all the paperwork and form filling that you have to do when you keep livestock. I did suggest at a Kerry Hill council meeting that perhaps we could cross our Kerry Hill sheep with elephants and kangaroos. My idea being that the babies born would have large enough ears to put the tags in and a pouch to carry all the paperwork.

What did the ram sing to the ewe when he fell in love?
   "There will never be another ewe."

When I was teaching I taught a knowledgeable farmer's son called David. His maths teacher asked him the following question:
   "If there are 50 sheep in a field and one gets out through the broken down fence how many sheep are left in the field?"
   "None," replied David.
   The teacher said, "You don't know maths do you?"
   "Sorry, Sir," said David, "but you don't know sheep."

A local sheep farmer kept a Border Collie with no legs.
   "What's the name of your collie?" I asked.

"I've forgotten but it doesn't matter because he doesn't come anyway," was his reply.

One of my friends bought a large, steel framed building with all the extras. After spending a vast amount of money, he had a slight problem during the first week of housing the ewes. Just at the wrong moment there was a power cut. He was just about to help a ewe that was in difficulty lambing when out went all the lights. He was accompanied by his four-year-old son, William. The two of them ran back to the house to fetch a torch and were soon back inside the shed ready to lamb the ewe.

"Hold the torch steady, son, hold the torch steady," said Harry and he soon brought out a live lamb.

"Hold the torch steady, son," he said and again Harry put his hand into the ewe and brought out another live lamb. The little boy was amazed.

"Hold the torch steady, son," Harry repeated and pulled out a third lamb and then a fourth. William was now totally amazed and stood with his mouth wide open.

"Do you think it's the light that's attracting them, Dad?" he asked.

Why did the ram jump off the cliff and kill himself?

He didn't see the ewe turn.

Bob, a sheep farmer I know very well, couldn't sleep at night. He of course tried counting sheep but that didn't work and so he eventually went to the doctor for some sleeping pills. The next morning I asked him how he had got on with his sleeping pills.

"Well, John, I got it totally wrong."

"Why is that?" I asked.

"I took the pills at 11.30pm with a cup of coffee – the coffee wouldn't let me sleep and the pills wouldn't let me stay awake – I didn't know if I was coming or going."

My farm boss needed some new trousers to wear during lambing. He went to the army and navy stores for some camouflage trousers but he couldn't find a pair.

Where does the ram get his raddle from?

A Tupperware party of course.

Note: A raddle is a harness which holds a pad of coloured wax called a crayon. The crayon sits between the front legs of the ram. When he serves the ewes they will have a coloured mark on their rumps. A tup is an alternative name for a ram.)

Sheep

A notice in the school dining room read:
"Every time a sheep baas it loses a mouthful."

Note: In other words you can't eat and talk at the same time.

A Birmingham teacher took her school children on a school visit to a livestock farm. The farmer explained that the lambing shed was seasonal; it was only used in the spring to house the in-lamb ewes and then the new born lambs with their mothers. For the rest of the year the building remained empty. The teacher asked one of her pupils to name the four seasons. Her answer was salt, pepper, mustard and vinegar!

Bob, a local sheep farmer, told me his faithful old collie, Jess, always slept in her basket in the farm kitchen.

"Where does the Rottweiler sleep?" I asked.

"Anywhere he wants to!" he replied.

Mary had a little lamb
Its fleece was white as snow
And everywhere that Mary went
The lamb was sure to go

Now Mary found the price of meat too high
Which really didn't please her
Tonight she's having leg of lamb
The rest is in the freezer.

The Royal mint is what the Queen puts on one's Royal lamb.

As former teachers, my wife Sarah and I are forever finding fault when we are out and about, finding spelling mistakes on menus and notices. We often want to reach for our red pens – old habits die hard. A genuine sign in a jewellers in Hinckley, Leicestershire says "Watch batteries fitted". I can honestly say I went into the shop and joked with them and said that I had got better things to do with my time! The notice is still there to this day. I have only ever seen one silly notice connected with farming, however, and this was at a farmer's mart. It read:

"Farmers with sheep in an intoxicated condition will not be allowed in the sale ring."

What did the cloned sheep say to the other sheep that looked the same as her?

I am ewe.

Feeding and looking after livestock is much easier when you are younger and as you get older it becomes harder to use a muck fork. A fellow that came to buy sheep off me to start his first flock asked me what qualifications I had got. I replied by telling him I had an M.Sc.

"What, a Master of Science?" he said.

"No," I replied. "A muck shovelling certificate!"

That's the end of this chapter so all's wool that ends wool.

To be continewe'd.

• 14 •

Farmers' Daughters

"I've sold all my sheep to pay for her wedding and now all I have got to give away is my daughter."

The farmer wanted to tidy up the farm and dispose of a lot of rubbish so he asked his daughter to telephone and order a skip.

She called a local firm and said, "I want a skip outside the barn please."

The fellow replied, "It's your farm, you can skip where you like!"

Mandy was stopped by the police travelling home from the office at the Farmer's Mart; she was certainly speeding. The policeman asked to see her driver's licence.

"What are you asking me that for? It was taken away from me yesterday and now you want to see it again!"

"Can I try that dress on in the window?"

A farmer's daughter went into town to buy a new dress for the Young Farmers' dance. She found a dress she liked in the window of a posh dress shop.

"Can I try that dress on in the window?"

"I would prefer it if you used the dressing room," was the shop assistant's reply.

The farmer's daughter, Jill was worried that she was pregnant and bought a twin pack pregnancy testing kit. Both tests were positive and so she told everyone she was having twins.

The farmer's wife said to her husband, "I am worried about our Shirley, she is too young to get married."

"Oh, don't worry, think of it like this – we are losing a daughter but we are gaining a bathroom!"

Pam's mother sent her to the fish and chip shop.

In the shop she asked, "Is this fish fresh?"

"Yes, madam."

"I thought so; it's just eaten my chips!"

A farmer's son was going out with a farmer's daughter. He had flying lessons and eventually bought a light aircraft.

"Come for a ride with me – it will be brilliant – we can even fly upside down."

"But we will fall out."

"No, we won't. I will still talk to you."

A farmer's wife was giving her daughter some advice.

"Love is whispering sweet nothings in your ear – marriage is sweet nothing in the bank.

Love is kissing on the sofa – marriage is deciding which sofa to buy.

Love is talking about producing some children – marriage is getting someone else to look after the children."

The farmer's daughter, Zoe, wasn't a good cook and usually let her mother do all the cooking. However, one day she had an accident opening a can of alphabet spaghetti.

"Did you hurt yourself?" asked her mother.

"No, but it could have spelt disaster!"

A farmer was worried about the number of bills coming in to the house and one day he noticed his daughter on the telephone for just over an hour.

"What's the matter?" he asked sarcastically. "You are usually on the telephone for at least two hours."

"It was a wrong number," was her reply.

"Dad, I've had a compliment on my driving – there was a note on my windscreen which said 'Parking fine' so I have got no worries there!"

Two farmers were talking at market: "I see your daughter has got a new boyfriend – another doctor!"

"I can't keep up with these boyfriends – she works at the hospital and has been taken out so many times by doctors they have nicknamed her Tonsil."

Dorothy, the farmer's wife, gave her daughter some advice:

"Claire, listen to me, some advice before you get married. Cook your husband a fish and it will keep him quiet for one meal but teach him how to fish and you just might get rid of him for the whole weekend!"

The farmer's daughter went to the doctors.

"Doctor, I have forgotten to take my contradictive pill."

The doctor replied, "You're ignorant."

She said, "Yes, three months!"

A farming couple are sadly at the divorce court.

"Why are you getting divorced?"

"We can't agree on anything at all," answered the fellow.

"How long has this gone on for?"

"Nine months," he replied.

"Ten months," snapped his wife!

The farming family were in the pub.

"Get a round of drinks in, Julie, please."

Julie went up to the bar. "Two pints of lager, a gin and tonic, a coke and an orange please."

"Still orange?" asked the barman.

"Yes, I haven't changed my mind!"

The farmer's daughter went to the garage and asked for a seven hundred and ten.

The mechanic scratched his head and said, "I have been a mechanic for 30 years and I've not heard of one. What does it look like?"

"It's a screw type cap thing that fits in the centre of the engine."

The mechanic was still none the wiser and gave her a pen and a piece of paper and said, "Draw it for me."

She drew a circle and put 710 in the middle of the circle.

The mechanic was still confused and opened up a bonnet of another car.

"Can you see one in there?" he asked.

"Yes, 710 there but it's upside down," the girl said pointing to the OIL cap.

My daughter was waiting for a bus. She missed the number 66 so she took the 33 twice.

The farmer's daughter, Julie, came home after a shopping trip.

"Did you buy a new dress, Julie?" asked her mother.

"No, but I found a lovely dress. It would have fitted me if I could have got into it!"

"My daughter is highly intelligent," said one livestock farmer at market.

"I wish mine was," said the other farmer. "She spent half an hour looking at her orange juice because it said 'concentrate'."

"I don't like your boyfriend. He is a scruffy individual, a waste of space and a real townie. He's no good for a farmer's daughter."

"But Dad, if he was no good why would he be doing all of this community service?"

The farmer's daughter couldn't sell her car; the 250,000 miles on the clock was putting people off. Her father told her he had a mate that could wind the clock back so she agreed and the clock was turned back to 40,000 miles.

A week later her father asked "Have you sold your car?"

"No, Dad. I'm not going to bother because it's only done 40,000 miles!"

A farmer's daughter put lipstick on her forehead because her father told her to make up her mind!

A week later her father asked "Have you sold your car?"
"No, Dad. I'm not going to bother because it's only done
40,000 miles!"

The farmer said to his daughter, "Look at that dog with one eye."

She covered up her eye with her hand and said, "Where?"

The day before her wedding the farmer said to his daughter, "In 50 years' time you will say this is the happiest day of your life."

"But Dad, I'm getting married tomorrow!"

"I know that," replied her Dad.

The daughter brought her boyfriend home to meet her father who was an arable farmer. After a while they announced their engagement.

After the boyfriend had left her father asked, "What does he do and has he any capital?"

"You men are all the same, Dad – that's what he asked about you."

The farmer's daughter went next door to baby sit their children. Their parents went out and the first thing she did was to herd them all up the stairs to bed and then she settled down to watch television. After ten minutes a little boy crept down the stairs.

"Go back upstairs at once," she said.

He did as he was told but he kept coming down the stairs every ten or fifteen minutes and he was sent back each time. Then there was a knock on the door.

"Is my son here?" asked the man at the door.

With that the little boy came down the stairs again.

"Dad, she won't let me come home!" he cried.

The farmer's daughter has swallowed a spoon and she hasn't stirred since!

Farmer Bill was worried about his daughter who hadn't got a job.

"Dad I've got a job at last – it's in a bowling alley."

"Ten pin?"

"No Dad, it's permanent!"

"My daughter has fallen out with her farmer boyfriend and is now going out with a plastic surgeon which has raised a few eyebrows!" reported the farmer to his mates at the pub.

The farmer told his daughter she needed to be stronger to work on the farm and perhaps she should do some exercises to build up her muscles. She wasn't keen on doing exercises so she went to the doctors and asked him if he could give her something to help. She was given some tablets for her strength but when she got home she couldn't get the top off the bottle.

• 15 •

Farm Students

I said to my old farm boss, "How is your new student coping with the hard work?"

"He gets tired brushing his teeth!" was his quick and short reply.

I told Peter in my agricultural class, "This project you have completed on the farm study is word for word the same as your brother's."

"Yes, Sir, it's the same farm," was his reply.

My farm student said to me, "My grandfather is a 91-year-old farmer and is still involved with a little of the day to day work on the farm. He is in good health and has never needed glasses."

"Well, that's marvellously good for him," I replied.

"No, Sir, he always drinks straight from the bottle," he said and chortled at his own cleverness.

The cross eyed lecturer at agricultural college couldn't control his pupils.

The agricultural lecturer said to her students, "The only way you are going to get straight As is to use a ruler!"

I always enjoyed teaching lessons involving livestock and I was proud we had a good range of livestock on our school farm including cattle.

During a question and answer session I had the following response to the question "Name six things that contain milk".

Jill replied, "Cheese, butter, ice cream, and three cows."

A notice in an examination room read: "Time will pass but will you?"

A student asked me if H_2O is water, what is H_2O_4?

"Tell me then please." I replied.

"To drink, to wash in and to swim in!"

During one of my question and answer sessions at school: "What is the meat of cattle called?"

"Beef," answered Amanda.

"Correct. What is the meat of calves called?"

"Veal," answered Matthew.

"Correct. What is cow hide used for?"

"To stop the cow falling apart," answered Joanne.

"Which is correct, but not the answer I was looking for," was my reply.

In the school dining room one of the dinner ladies put a note on the bowl containing the apples that read "Take one apple only, God is watching you".

At the end of the counter, past the rest of the food, was a pile of chocolate biscuits. One of the students had written another note and placed it in front of the plate. It read, "Take as many chocolate biscuits as you want because God is watching the apples"!

"Where's your farming project, Samantha?" I asked.

"It's at home, Sir."

"What's it doing there?"

"Having a better day than me!"

"If I am gorgeous which tense is that?" she asked.

An agricultural lecturer at farming college was due to retire and she was appalled at some students in her class because their basic English skills were poor.

"If I am gorgeous which tense is that?" she asked.

The student answered, "Past tense, Miss, past tense."

During a lesson on fruit and vegetables I was asked, "Sir, if you take a pumpkin and divide its circumference by the diameter, do you get pumpkin Pi?"

What happened to all the pot plants sitting on the window sill in the agricultural statistics class?

They developed square roots.

Answers from examination questions:

1 What is a fibula?
  Answer: a small lie.

2 Name one way to stop milk turning sour.
  Answer: keep it in the cow.

3 Describe ten animals that live on a farm.
   Answer: six cows and four sheep.

4 Metric: – change centimetres to metres.
   Answer: delete the first five letters (centi).

At the agricultural sports day Peter Jones was easily winning the 100 metres race but got an apple seed in his eye and so he was pipped at the post.

"Why are you late again, Simon?"
   "But it's never too late to learn, Sir!"

One of my agricultural students, Robert, was a good, hard working lad in my lessons but he was often in trouble with the headmaster.

   "Robert, I saw you leaving the headmaster's office again this morning. Was he telling you off for being late again?" I asked.

   "Yes, Sir."

   "And what excuse did you give this time?"

   "As you know, Sir, we have to drive along the new bypass to get to school."

   "Yes, I know that."

   "Well, Sir, a lorry carrying glue had tipped over."

"Was anyone hurt?"

"No, Sir, but we all had to stick to the inside lane."

I couldn't help laughing.

"Come to think of it I saw you arriving at school in a brand new sports car so you shouldn't be late."

"Yes, Sir, but I arrive late much faster now!"

"Oh, go and sit down."

"David, you know you can't sleep in my class."

"Not at the moment, Sir, but if you talked a little quieter I could!"

Mr Martin was a good maths teacher and he often brought agriculture or horticulture examples to use in his maths class.

He asked Lynne Robinson, "If you cut a banana into ten pieces, an apple into four pieces and a pear into two pieces, what do you get?"

"A fruit salad," was her reply.

The farmer asked his student a technical question.

"What is nitrate?"

"Double time I hope," was the student's reply.

Unfortunately a big lad fell through a crack in the floor boards.

Farm Students

At the agricultural college the students had put on a production of Shakespeare. Unfortunately a big lad fell through a crack in the floor boards.

The college principal rushed on and told the audience not to worry, it was just a stage he was going through.

I caught Tim, one of my students, feeding the milk back to Anna, our goat, just after milking her. It was a cold January morning and she could not drink it fast enough, it was lovely and warm.

"What are you doing feeding the milk back to the goat?" I asked, "We could be selling that at 25p a pint."

"I'm sorry, Sir," he stuttered. "I got a bit of muck in the milk so I am just running it through her again for you."

A farmer's son in my class told me his father was not well and he had been to the doctors.

"What did he say?"

"He said he must exercise with dumb-bells."

"Is he?"

"Well, he's been for a walk with his new girlfriend."

Harry's father was a magician.

"What's his best trick?" the farmer asked.

"Sawing people in half," was his reply.

"Have you got any brothers or sisters?"

"Yes, one half brother and two half-sisters."

When a teacher is absent from school due to illness or attending a course, a teacher with a free period will take the lesson or a supply teacher is brought in. One day at my school, a certain lady teacher was absent and so the headmaster decided to take the lesson.

"What do pigs give you?"

"Pork, sir."

"Correct. What do sheep give you?"

"Lamb and wool, sir."

"Correct. What does the fat cow give you?"

"Homework, sir."

A pupil on the telephone to the school secretary said: "My son has a bad cold and will be absent from school for the rest of the week."

The secretary said, "Who is this?"

The student replied, "This is my father speaking."

I asked a student, "Name four members of the dog family."

The answer came, "Father, mother and two puppies."

When I went for my interview for my first full time job on a farm I was firstly shown the farm buildings and finally the workers' toilet.

"This is the workers' toilet," said the boss, pushing the door open.

"But there's no lock on the door," I observed.

"No problem mate," he replied. "Nobody's ever stolen the bucket!"

The head master called Ryan into his office.

"Your agriculture is good but in English you use two words too often. One is great and one is lousy."

"Certainly, Sir – but what are they?"

A lady that was a student at a certain midlands Agricultural College 30 years ago visited the vets. Above the door on his consulting room was his name, Clive Roberts MRCVS.

I was at college with a Clive Roberts, she thought, and when she went into the consulting room with her dog she thought she recognised him but instead of being that good looking handsome fellow he was very old and wrinkled.

She asked him if he was at that same College 30 years ago.

"Yes," he replied.

"So was I," she said excitedly thinking that she had aged better than him.

"What subject did you teach?" he asked.

The agricultural teacher told the lad off because he said, "I ain't got a pencil, Miss."

"Let me explain, we will put it in better English. David hasn't got a pencil, Julia hasn't got a pencil and Sarah has got no pencils at all."

"So who's got all the pencils, Miss?" he asked.

What did the agricultural science lecturer say to the hydrogen atom that had lost an electron?

"Are you positive?"

Two farming students were arguing and then started fighting. The lady teacher was appalled at their behaviour and took them into her office.

"What's this all about?" she asked sternly.

One lad answered her, "We found a £10 note and we were having a competition to see who could tell the biggest lie – the winner would get the £10."

"I am so ashamed," she said. "When I was your age I knew how to behave and I didn't know what a lie was."

The boys looked at each other and gave the £10 to the lady teacher.

One of my former students, a farmer's daughter, works in a cafe.

I went in and asked, "What milk shakes have you got?"

She said, "Raspberry and vanilla," in a very croaky voice.

"Have you got laryngitis?" I asked.

"No, just raspberry and vanilla," she replied.

Richard Keightley was one of my less able students and had a habit of getting things very wrong. I taught a lesson on how important it is to encourage wild birds onto the farm and I thought my lesson on migration was good. The following week I asked Richard what was meant by migration. There was a long silence while Richard gazed into space seeking inspiration. The process looked positively painful. He screwed up his face, grimaced and looked to be in agony, such was his concentration.

"Well . . . I'm not exactly sure, Sir, but I think 'migration' is when my mum gets those bad headaches."

Wise Words

A farmer friend told me to learn how to cut my fingernails with my left hand in case I lost the right one.

Farming is hard work and in all weathers. A neighbouring dairy farmer has always worked hard and when his son left school he joined his father on the farm. They worked 12 hours a day, seven days a week and after six years his son asked for a Sunday afternoon off work. His father's reply was, "Why? Are you not happy in your work?"

Some farmers pay their bills when they are due, some pay when they are overdue and some never do.

Poultry are the only farm animals you can eat before they are born and after they are dead.

"If you break anything or you forget to do something you must tell me – we have no secrets here because the potatoes have eyes and the corn has ears."

Rumours on a farm are not necessarily true but they often go in one ear and in another.

There are three types of people that you have to deal with when you are a farmer: left handed, right handed and under handed.

The early bird catches the worm but the mouse that arrives second on the scene will get the cheese.

How do you make a small fortune in farming?
    Start with a large fortune.

A quote from a farmer:
    "I don't have to farm for a living, I just carry on so that I can afford luxuries such as bread, potatoes, some vegetables and a pair of shoes."

The farm boss talking to his new member of staff:

"Work hard, don't forget I am the only person on this farm that watches the clock on your tea break and dinner break."

A farmer makes a small amount of money on the farm and spends it in town on groceries.

A city gent makes his money in town and spends it all on the farm.

I said to my farm boss, "You are lucky in that your workers on this farm always seem to be working very hard."

His reply was, "When they come for their interview for the job I always tell them that my watch passes the time by keeping its hands busy."

It is much better for a farmer to have his hands on a lady than a lady on his hands.

"Do we get a tea break?" asked the new farm worker.

"Yes, we do. On this farm we drink our tea out of cups and on the next door farm they drink their tea out of doors," replied the boss.

Farmer's wives that are good at dressmaking will sew what they gather and their husbands will gather what they sow.

Two thirds of farmers don't know how the other half lives.

A successful farmer is a man who makes lots more money than his wife can spend.

A successful woman is someone who can find such a man.

It is hard to find a farmer who is poor, but there are certainly many poor farmers.

Farmers earn a small celery, come home beet, like to read the pepper, turn-ip the covers endive into bed.

In farming everybody knows more than somebody but nobody knows more than everybody.

It's easy enough to be pleasant when the world rolls along like a song, but a farmer's worthwhile if he can smile when everything's going wrong.